JAPANESE
FLOWER ARRANGEMENT

Also by Mary Badham Kittel

Easy Ways to Good Flower Arrangement

JAPANESE

Flower Arrangement

FOR AMERICAN HOMES

BY

Mary Badham Kittel

BONANZA BOOKS · New York

ACKNOWLEDGMENTS

The author wishes to thank the authors and publishers for permission to use photographs from the following publications: *Design for Flower Arrangers* by Dorothy W. Riester (Van Nostrand Co., Inc.); *Design and Depth in Flower Arrangement* by Emma Hodkins Cyphers (Hearthside Press, Inc.); *Flower Show Ribbon Winning Arrangements*, Mrs. Raymond Russ Stoltz, Scribner Publications, Inc.; *The Flower Arrangement Calendar*, 1959 by Helen Van Pelt Wilson, M. Barrows & Company, Inc.; *The New York Times*; and *The National Gardener*, bulletin of the National Council of State Garden Clubs, Inc.

The author is also grateful to Herbert Reid, Scott Fikes, and Frank Karr for expert help on art work; to Mary Umsted; and to Lirl Treuter of the Fort Worth Public Library; as well as to Mesdames Yoneo Arai, T. Yamamoto, Josui Oshikawa, Kiyoaki Saibara, and Warren Saibara; to Yashiko Saito, Dusty Aono, Buddy Benz, Musanobu Kudo, and Houn Ohara for valuable assistance on research work; to Del Beavers, Mattie Mae Bennett, Hope Montanez, and Marjorie Gillum for patience and help in preparing the manuscript; and particularly to Esther Wheeler for the loan of containers, as well as her home in Roslyn Heights, Long Island, New York, as a background for arrangements shown on pages 39, 79, 87, 89, 93, 101, 102, and 151.

Contents

To TRUDE

who doesn't know (and doesn't want to know!)
a rose from a petunia, but somehow intuitively
knew when I was too busy to remember food.

Foreword

Where flowers are arranged with thought and care there is usually some evidence of the principles taught by the Japanese masters. The influence of the Orient is sometimes great, sometimes slight, but today the most effective flower designs of the Occident express the simplicity advocated by the Japanese for hundreds of years.

The Oriental art of flower arranging is based on features that carry deep spiritual significance. Every branch and flower, every line has special meaning. However, to most flower arrangers outside the Orient, the underlying esoteric ideas are of much less importance than the techniques employed in the creation of these beautiful designs. Certainly it is not necessary to study Oriental symbolism in order to make an arrangement in the Rikkwa, Ikenobo, or Nageire style. Yet by reading about the deeper aspects of Japanese flower arrangement we can at once appreciate the heights of subtlety to which the Oriental masters have raised this fascinating art. The assimilation of their teachings about expressiveness of line, composition, and the subtle use of color have led many flower arrangers into painting and interior decoration as well as other arts.

The ancient Japanese masters of flower arrangement have given us a blueprint or guide, founded on universal art principles. And if we learn a few of the basic rules we can create distinctive designs for any type of room, using materials that are most readily at our disposal. This is the underlying theme of the present book.

The "non-realistic" or "free-style" designs which many of the modern Japanese schools incorporate into their teachings are not part of our study. Although these designs are often thought-provoking, most of them can hardly be classed as "flower arrangements." Iron, string, tin, rags, pottery, and even Styrofoam are often featured without any plant material at all. When flowers *are* included in these "abstractions" they are usually distorted or placed contrary to nature (so "the flower will not know it is a flower"), while dried branches and roots may be painted red, yellow, or purple and even turned upside down (so the tree "will not remember its growing").

[7]

The struggle for originality throughout the ages has frequently led to writing which says little or nothing, music which is more noise than melody, and paintings which are beyond reasonable interpretation even by their perpetrators. The new type of Japanese flower arranging goes along with other contemporary arts in minimizing the need to be intelligible. However, most recognized schools do require that when placed on exhibit such compositions be given titles or theme names.

While modern Japan has discarded much of her conservatism, floral artists disagree as to whether this revolutionary expression of imaginary forms is just a passing fad. In any case, well-established schools do not advocate that the student branch out into the abstract forms before mastering the basic principles of the art. Like teachers of painting or music, the Japanese masters of flower arrangement insist first on a fundamental knowledge of classic traditions and rules. Once these have been understood, sensible and effective adaptations can be made as the flower arranger continues to experiment.

Simplicity has always marked the arts of Japan. The country's best-loved paintings consist of a few rhythmic lines, dexterously set down on paper or silk; her favorite poems contain only a well-chosen phrase or two; and her drama is a study in restrained but very expressive movement. The art of Japan leans heavily upon suggestion, stimulating and directing the imagination through simple understatement—encouraging observers to discover extra "concealed beauty" for themselves.

The flower master practices to develop manual skill and efficiency in technique, but underlying this aim is the cultivation of a closer unity with nature and a deeper love of beauty. This, people of all countries understand. Flower arrangement is a means of self-expression which also provides satisfying beauty for the adornment of the home. It is easy to understand why, in this design-conscious age, it has become such a popular form of art.

[8]

JAPANESE
FLOWER ARRANGEMENT

I: **IKENOBO**

Variations on a Formal Theme

Contrary to general opinion, classic Japanese flower arrangements are simple to make. Their construction, based on efficient handling, produces the longest-lasting results possible with cut material. A third practical reason for making such designs—quite apart from their beauty—lies in the comparatively small amount of material required.

Twelve centuries of regimentation, set up by dedicated students of nature, have given us certain rules to follow. These rules do not, as one might suppose, lead to sameness of design. Every gardener knows that flowers from the same plant can be as provocatively different as human beings. And it follows that this must be equally true in their arrangement, since the wide variety of materials and combinations of materials allows for an infinite number of effects within any set pattern.

The goal of the Japanese flower master is to accentuate and idealize the individuality of each plant, *not* to destroy it. He may skillfully bend a branch to his will, but only to re-create a vital moment of arrested growth typical of that particular plant.

A quick glance at an illustration of a traditional Japanese arrangement and one made in the old European manner will point up the Oriental respect for the beauty of each individual stem, leaf, and flower, as well as the European love of opulence typified in the massing of bloom to produce a single showy burst of color which conceals the shape of individual flowers and stems.

In Japanese flower arrangement the growth line is extremely important. Blossoms and foliage are considered embellishments of this line and are therefore never massed in a way that would compete with or hide its beauty. When painting a picture, artists control the use of color in order to strengthen the over-all design; similarly, sculptors sacrifice much of a piece of marble's beauty in order to emphasize the theme of their compositions. The Oriental flower masters teach equal restraint in the use of flowers. The idea, or inner meaning, is the essence of design in any art form, and Japanese flower arranging is an art—not a craft.

In developing their rules, the Japanese flower masters were guided first of all by basic art principles; they also studied the growth habits of plants under all weather conditions; then, by arranging similar cut material over and over again, they gradually arrived at certain standard practices. These were passed down from generation to generation.

Ikebana is a general term for all forms of flower arranging and may be freely translated as "flowers arranged according to a certain order or method." (Literal translations are variously given as "living flowers," "growing flowers," "orderly flowers," "flowers that grow," etc.) This "orderly" treatment stemmed from sixth-century priests who, feeling it was neither reverent nor dignified to offer flowers carelessly to Buddha, adapted Chinese art principles to the Japanese love of nature and devised formal floral offerings.

Although *shin-no-hana*, or "altar arrangements," were, it appears, stylized long before William the Conqueror in the eleventh century, Ikebana did not penetrate to the people until 1500 A.D., when Sen-no-Kikyu introduced bamboo containers. (Fifty-odd varieties of bamboo grow in Japan.) Prior to that time the fine arts were confined to priests, warriors, and the nobility; it was not until early in the twentieth century that women became active in the art. Ikebana is now practiced by all classes and there are well over thirty thousand registered teachers in Tokyo alone.

Like most formal arts—music, painting, and sculpture, as well as architecture—the basic form evolved through religion. In arranging flowers, the Japanese priests followed the same vibrant rhythmic lines popularly employed in the sister arts of painting and sculpture. Although history reveals many different schools, their chief differences lay in terminology and types of containers, holders, and material which were considered correct. So closely related is this art to the life of the people that historians trace the thought currents of the race through names used by these schools to designate the various lines or levels of material.

Ikenobo, "hermitage by—or of—the lake," is said to be the school from which all others stemmed. We are told that it was founded by Ono-no-Imoko more than fourteen hundred years ago. In 552 A.D. he was sent to the court of China by his cousin, the prince regent, to make a study of Buddhism and the arts which it fostered. Ono-no-Imoko's particular interest lay in flowers, and although history records Japanese gardens prior to the sixth century the idea of incorporating a lake or pond was brought back from China by him. When his benefactor died he retired to a small hut beside one of his garden lakes to pray for the repose of the prince's soul. As was the Buddhist custom, he shaved his head and spent his days in meditation, holding services each morning and evening before the tablet of his friend.

An increasing number of students attended these services, seeking cultural guidance from a member of the imperial family who had studied in China. As time went on Ono-no-Imoko gave up material interests and applied himself exclusively to meditation and study. He died at the age of eighty-eight, leaving many students who had not only learned the mysteries of the new religion from him, but had also studied his form of floral offering. After returning to their communities, these priests used rituals similar to those in the "hermitage by the lake," thus giving a name to the first flower-arranging school.

When Ono-no-Imoko gave up worldly affairs to devote his life to the priesthood he changed his name to Senmu, and as his son and his son's sons took over the duties of priest and master they also changed their names to some form of Sen. The forty-fifth generation of Sen teaches in the same place today. The well that is said to have supplied water for the original lake is still in use, and tradition claims that the small six-sided temple in Kyoto (present headquarters of the Ikenobo school) is built on the ancient lake site.

Although many schools had early beginnings, during the latter half of the fifteenth century Senjun, twenty-sixth master of Ikenobo, was given the title of *Iemoto* or head-master of all flower-arrangement teaching in Japan. The Iemoto, "root-house" of an art, or method of teaching, is granted the sole power of issuing diplomas for work done by his followers. Once granted, this authority is never lost for, if there is no son, the Iemoto appoints a favorite student as his successor. The thousands of Ikenobo teachers throughout Japan register their students at the Ikenobo headquarters in Kyoto and examiners from Kyoto go to the larger cities at stated intervals to test the students' ability. When a diploma is issued the student also receives a flower name incorporating a syllable of the teacher's name.

Each successive master of Ikenobo has contributed to the accumulated knowledge, yet an unpracticed eye finds little difference between the classic designs of today and those of three hundred years ago. The teachings still include rules of conduct and stress the necessity for a proper mental attitude; experts claim they can recognize the artist's state of mind by his arrangement. Be that as it may, the number of students in this school is said to equal that of all other schools combined.

Early teachings were passed on by word of mouth, so there are no written records showing the form taken by those first offerings. However, we are told that the sturdy pine of the native Japanese ritual was used as a background for the short-lived blossoms employed in Buddhist ceremonies. The beauty of bright-hued flowers was not neglected, but was subordinated to longer-lasting tree branches. This idea of representing the universal life as opposed to man's short span is as popular today as when it was first used by earnest students in the "hermitage by the lake" so many centuries ago. (It was the forerunner of our own long-lasting arrangements, with easily changed centers of interest.)

The Ikenobo curves and proportions govern all other "realistic" forms, regardless of the school or master. Three main lines, joined at the base and presenting the appearance of a living, growing unit, are stressed. These lines—or groups of lines—are complete in themselves, yet each conforms to the whole. This graceful tree form is used both with and without a "root-hider" of flowers at its feet.

Kobori-Enshiu, a renowned art connoisseur, tea master, and designer of gardens, founded the *Enshiu* school in the sixteenth century. He exaggerated the sweeping Ikenobo curves and adapted them to containers which were quite small in relation to the plant material. Accepted harmonious proportions were maintained through specially designed tables and flower stands (the beginning of our present-day bases).

These rhythmic designs were set off by small, exquisitely proportioned bronze containers which represented the trunk of the tree. Placed on tall, slender-legged tables, the

Nine palmetto fronds, clipped and shaped to Ikenobo proportions, arranged in a vertical black container on a teak base. The classic "earth" line (Tai) at lower right follows the prescribed Enshiu placement by curving around from behind the main or "heaven" line (Shin), which emerges in an unbroken curve from the container. The "man" (Soe) placement, branching to the left, is the third part of the traditional Japanese composition. Black pebbles cover the needlepoint holder.

The container, handsome enough for the formal design, was actually made at home with the help of a Pilsner glass and a cracked phonograph record! The record, placed in a warm oven (with the door open) on top of a deep saucer, was allowed to sag slightly from the heat, then was molded into shape with glove-covered hands and glued to the bottom of the glass. The hole and cracks were sealed with paraffin. Several sprayings with waterproof black paint completed the job.

Palm seems a happy choice for such a container since it symbolizes self-education! (Photo: Lawrence Joseph.)

The heavy base used under the container and the strong nemoto (root or trunk) arranged in it help balance this tall Ikenobo design. The pine branch was trimmed, each cluster of needles being shortened and carefully thinned to add to the ruggedness and apparent size of the "tree." Small sweetheart roses were arranged to look like a bush growing at its feet.

Pine will stay green for weeks if the ends of heavy stems are split or crushed (for better water absorption) and branches submerged in deep water for several hours before the arrangement is made. When the roses begin to droop they can be replaced with new ones or any seasonal flower small enough to act as a similar foil for the "tree."

Because of its sturdiness and vigorous evergreen needles, and also because the tree is often associated with mist, rain, sea, and mountains, pine symbolizes many things to the Japanese —long life, courage, loyalty, faithfulness, strength, endurance, steadfastness, health, and prosperity. Gnarled pine is considered particularly manly—at times like an austere, aged hero with great strength of character, unmoved by the affairs of puny men, or like a giant with muscular arms and legs, standing supreme over all it surveys.

Pine is also likened to the life of the race (strong and eternal), while the rose (used in combination with it here) symbolizes the mortal and temporal life of the individual. In Japan, any evergreen-tree branches and cut flowers can be used to express eternal youth and everlasting spring, but pine is highly favored. (Photo: Lawrence Joseph.)

[16]

"trees," expressing fluidity of line, soared to astounding heights while maintaining perfect balance. Although it adhered strictly to classic lines and many taboos, the Enshiu school introduced the use of "nanten" or "heavenly bamboo," as well as seeds and fruits. (Nandina is now permitted by Ikenobo followers, but fruit branches are still allowed only when in bloom.)

Even though flower arranging started as an accessory to religion, it soon took on metaphysical and historical associations. Particularly popular are religious and secular ideas which relate human experience to the rhythm of the universe. Emotion, physical characteristics, weather conditions, time, and place, are all subtly indicated by the choice of material, the directions taken by the lines, and the angles formed by them. The flowing lines interpret love of nature in all its manifestations. They suggest the orderly progress of the seasons, telling of life and death, cause and result, and play an important part in any home or national celebration such as marriage, birth, graduation, or New Year's. Every phase of plant life is so laden with meaning that even a painter would hesitate to paint a flower out of season!

Japanese culture lays as much stress on developing kindly qualities of the heart as it does on improving the mind, mixing the practical and poetic so that there is no clear distinction between art and life. The Japanese respect the beauty of nature as they do the good deeds of man, and flowers to them are an even more acceptable art medium than paint or stone. Much of the meaning behind the world's great paintings is lost to posterity, and although the Greeks carved their racial ideals in timeless marble only fragments survive. Yet flower arranging, which is a transitory medium, has long been and remains a vital force in the lives of the Japanese people. Private and public exhibits (much like recitals given by our music teachers) are every-day occurrences; factories, department stores, and large restaurants employ recognized flower-arranging teachers and allow time off for study; schools suspend classes and entire villages close up shop so that everyone may take advantage of special excursion rates and go chrysanthemum-viewing, iris-viewing, lotus-viewing, or even snow-viewing! (For a pine may be truly interpreted only by those who study *all* its aspects.) One reliable source reports five thousand people enjoying the mystic beauty of an old cherry tree bathed in moonlight!

It follows that arrangements by such people stem from an understanding of, as well as a love for, nature. They strive to express a state of idealized living—not colorful dying—because vitality is supremely important to them. This Shinto dislike of anything suggesting death made it difficult to accept the Buddhist ritual of scattering flower petals before sacred images. The idea of offering imperfect, mutilated blossoms to their gods was repugnant to the Japanese, so they compromised by substituting bits of colored paper—and thus confetti was born.

To the Oriental, the charm of a tilted leaf embodies cosmic verities. The delightfully opposed color and textural relationship between upper (male) and under (female) sides of the leaf is a constant reminder of the necessary balance between the two great forces regulating and responsible for all life. *Yang* and *Ying* (Chinese) and *In* and *Yo* (Japanese) are loosely equivalent to *any* strong contrast (such as masculine-feminine, left-right, light-dark, positive-negative).

[18]

The balance of these inequalities creates beauty by abolishing the weakness and monotony evident in symmetry. Making a symmetrical arrangement to the Japanese would be like digging a straight ditch in a garden rather than emphasizing the natural beauty of a meandering stream. Our uniformly made dishes and plates lack beauty to them for, conditioned as they are to entrancingly varied mountains, jagged coastline, and rocky terrain, beauty is apparent only in irregularity. Much of their floral symbolism is based on the fact that, while plants change with the season, their innate nature remains unchanged. A pine in the mist does not become a willow, nor does the most warlike samurai lose his love for the quietude of nature. These two sides of existence (changing and unchanging) are the balance point in any well-rounded life—or arrangement of flowers.

Man, when ruled by one-sided passion, loses this balance with nature. Plants and trees, however, being innocent and free of egotism, experience neither doubt, avarice, wickedness, nor malice, thereby remaining natural and reasonable—or well-balanced!

The terminology of various schools differs, but the fundamental thought, as well as the basic form, remains unchanged. The universe or nature itself is represented. Heaven, the soul of all things, earth, the way through which all things take form, and man, the fundamental way through which all things become active, are interpreted as heaven, man, and earth; principal, soul, and body; father, mother, and child; sun, moon, and earth; etc. *Any* cosmic unity showing three widely different elements, independent but necessary to each other and indispensable to the perfect whole, may be used to point up man's part in the trinity of the universe.

Every art has its basic form; Japanese arrangements, though conforming to nature's molds for individual stem, leaf, and flower patterns, are built on variations of this cosmic triangle. As in a novel or on the stage, the principal figures must not be eclipsed by the supporting characters, and if a teacher wishes to indicate this error he will politely inquire of the offending line, "Who is this?" (Never would he make the mistake of even thinking, "What is this?" for the line is too rife with symbolic meaning to be thought of impersonally.)

However, much to the Occidental student's confusion, nature is recognized as a notorious rule-breaker and, in order to point a moral, the natural beauty of some fantastic quirk may take precedence over the accepted order and, contrary to its own nature, peacefully mix up heaven, man, and earth!

In Ikenobo arrangements the stems are held firmly and invisibly together at the mouth of the container, rising naturally and beautifully, as a plant or tree springs from the earth. The lines express, even exaggerate, natural characteristics, as certain notes in music are accentuated to emphasize rhythm. The graceful droop of forsythia, the austere erectness of spuria iris, the dramatic angularity of pine, the length and movement of jointed grass, the exaggerated height of wild asters, the flowing grace of wisteria and morning glory—all are expressed by the character of the central or main line. As this line varies, so must the other lines vary in order to maintain consistent harmony of contrast and balance.

Once a single basic design is mastered it becomes a simple matter to adjust the curves, and the length of the other lines, to those of the central line. However, the Japanese flower master knows every variation so well that the instant he picks up a stem, several possible patterns leap into his mind. When he selects a suitable design all dimensions are instantly established for him.

There is style and elegance in height, and the height of the main line in an Ikenobo arrangement may vary from one and a half times the height of the container to six or even seven times. It is governed not only by the visual weight of container and material, but by habit of growth, season, and the purpose for which the arrangement is intended.

Ikenobo arrangements look best in dark bronze or other handsome, mellow containers, just as a dignified painting looks best in an elegant frame of subdued tone. Decoration on the container should be subordinate to form, and floral material should conform to the line of the container so that at first glance the eye is conscious only of the over-all design. The correct relationship between floral material and container is likened by the Japanese to rightness of dress for an important occasion.

Radiation from a seen or known point is the secret of vitality in all graphic arts, and the three ascending Ikenobo curves start a rhythmic movement like a musical beat. These three structural units, radiating in easy fluency from the point of diversion, may be arranged to mold any expression of a living plant into visual form. If the stems are to emphasize a dignified vertical (*Shin*, or formal) feeling, the main line should be curved like a gracefully standing man. If a flowing informal (*So*) arrangement is desired the main line should have the freedom of a running man; while the intermediate treatment for a semi-formal (*Gyo*) arrangement should suggest a man walking. (See diagram I-C on page 23.)

Three well-proportioned lines are often enough to satisfy the feeling for mass, height, design, movement, and interest, provided that the lines are closely united at the base and that spaces between the lines, as well as the angles at diversion, are bold and gracefully varied. Satisfactory results hinge as much upon these angles and spaces as upon the lines themselves, for voids play as important a part in the Ikenobo school as the pauses or rests in a musical score.

Construction Details Based on Ikenobo Rules

It is true that we in the West like to feel freer in the arrangement of flowers than classic Japanese rules permit. We enjoy adapting Ikenobo methods and we even go so far as to combine Oriental principles with period European designs to create what are now popularly called "line-mass" arrangements. But before mixing one style with another or trying to evolve an individual technique, everyone who enjoys handling flowers should at least know how a Japanese flower arrangement is made.

[20]

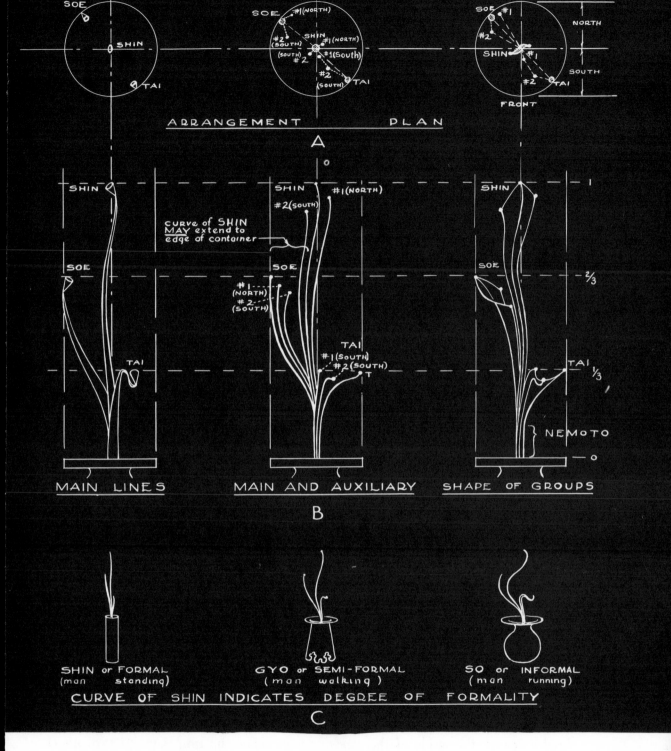

SOE

SHIN

TAI

SOE · #1 (NORTH)

#2 (SOUTH) · #1 (NORTH) · SHIN

#1 (South) · #2

#2 (SOUTH) · TAI

SOE · #1

#2 · NORTH

SHIN · #1 · SOUTH

#2 · TAI

FRONT

ARRANGEMENT PLAN

A

SHIN

#1 (NORTH)

#2 (SOUTH)

curve of SHIN MAY extend to edge of container

SOE

#1 (NORTH)

#2 (SOUTH)

TAI

#1 (SOUTH)

#2 (SOUTH)

T

SHIN

SOE

TAI

NEMOTO

2/3

1/3

o

MAIN LINES   MAIN AND AUXILIARY   SHAPE OF GROUPS

B

SHIN or FORMAL (man standing)

GYO or SEMI-FORMAL (man walking)

SO or INFORMAL (man running)

CURVE OF SHIN INDICATES DEGREE OF FORMALITY

C

DIAGRAM I

1. *Cutting the three main lines.*

Establish a gracefully curved half-moon or bow-shaped main line which follows these rules:

    (a) It should conform to the natural growth habit of the plant material.

    (b) It should be subtly allied to the shape and visual weight of the container. (The base or stand is considered an integral part of the composition.)

    (c) It should conform to the general shape, as well as the dimensions, of the space for which the arrangement is intended.

This main line varies in length from one and one-half times the height of the container to five or even six times its height. The taller the line, the more dramatic the arrangement; however, its length must be compatible with (a), (b), and (c) above.

Cut a second line two-thirds the length of the first and cut a third line one-third the length of the first, bearing in mind that if stems are to be bent to emphasize curves their lengths will be changed somewhat in the process. The one-third relationship of these lines must be *apparent* (seldom actual) for correct proportions. The greater the curve, the longer the stem must be cut.

The three main lines are *Shin*, *Soe*, and *Tai*. (See diagram I-B.) The English translations of the words are heaven, man, and earth, respectively. In garden-club circles the Japanese designation and the English translation are employed about equally.

2. *Strengthening the three main lines.*

In selecting stems or branches to support or strengthen these three basic groups, hold each group in the hand, remembering these suggestions:

    (a) As in a picture or piece of sculpture, the eye must be able to follow the main lines of the design comfortably, without distraction.

    (b) Each bloom should represent a formally placed ornament, and the slender lines should not therefore be overloaded with heavy spots of color.

    (c) Ikenobo is a sweeping, classic design form which expresses the beauty of nature through three carefully planned triangular and tridimensional groups.

3. *Holding the stems in place.*

The *kubari* or *matagi* is a Y-shaped stick used for holding stems in the correct position. This device often proves difficult for inexperienced arrangers; however, when used in conjunction with a needlepoint holder it is simple to handle and very helpful in keeping stems close together at the mouth of the container. (Diagram II-A.)

The kubari should be placed one-half inch below the surface of the water, with the bottom of the Y toward the arranger. For best results use a viscous branch (one that yields under stress without breaking) of apple, peach, willow, or cypress, about the size of the heaviest lead pencil, with a narrowly spreading Y. (The point of the Y should be large enough to receive stems placed in front of Shin, which, in Ikenobo arrangements, is always the central stem.)

Beveling the top ends of the Y slightly toward the outside will allow the kubari to fit firmly in a round container. First of all, cut the single end of the Y, and then hold it against the inside of the vase one inch below the rim; then cut two prongs

[22]

where they rest on the opposite rim. Make each cut in a slightly oblique direction (to conform to the shape of the vase) with the upper ends a trifle longer than the lower ones. If held in this slanting position (*not* horizontally) the kubari will not be too short. (If it is a little too long, the ends can be filed off with a fingernail file.)

After cutting the Y to required length, place its upper ends one inch below the water line against the inside wall of the container and, squeezing the ends of the Y together with the left hand, force the single end down gradually with right thumb until the kubari is horizontal. The double ends of the Y may then be forced open with a closed pair of shears. The holder should be so firmly fixed that it can be used as a handle for picking up the container.

If no natural Y of required size and shape is available, one can easily be made, as shown in diagram II-A, and inserted as described above.

It should be stressed again that only a snug-fitting kubari is successful. However, since wood expands with moisture, care must be exercised when using either pottery or glass containers, as there is always the danger of breakage. Allow a little leeway for expansion or soak the kubari in water overnight before fitting it into the vase.

The *usubata*, originally designed for Ikenobo arrangements, *requires* a kubari for best results. Usubatas, customarily made of bronze, come in many shapes and sizes; their distinguishing feature is a (usually removable) saucer-like top incorporating a flange or well for holding water.

A properly made kubari will last indefinitely. If it dries out and shrinks it needs only to be soaked in warm water overnight and worn ends padded with adhesive tape to assure a snug fit.

When using heavy branches in an arrangement, cut the ends of the stems on a slant and criss-cross them with shallow cuts so they will hold firmly to the needles of the holder. These stems should be forced onto the holder with a swaying motion before being braced against the kubari, which will give them additional support.

The *komi* is a small stick or wedge used behind stems for bracing them firmly in the crotch of the Y. This stick will hold better if cut straight across one end and square on the other. (See diagram II-A.)

4. Shin (heaven)

This is the main or tallest line of the arrangement. Any stem or branch used for the main line must be shaped so that its tip curves directly over the point where the stem leaves the container. (Curving tips are a *must* for obtaining proper visual balance in Ikenobo arrangements.) Branches may be bent between fingers and thumbs. With hands close together, press thumbs flat against the underside of the branch as your fingers work along the top of it, bending and smoothing the branch into the curve you need. Bend the main stem two inches below center (approximately one-half of the distance from the mouth of the container to the tip); then, two-thirds of the distance from the first bend to the tip, bend the branch back in the opposite direction. For best results and to prevent breakage, twist the branch slightly while bending and work only between buds and leaf nodules. When the curve is completed, the branch should lie flat on the table in a graceful bow shape.

[23]

On a heavy branch, a few shallow cuts made slantingly across the outside of the curve will usually be sufficient to make the branch hold the shape you want. In more obstinate cases, small wedges can be made and inserted in the cuts as shown in diagram II-B. This procedure insures a permanently curved branch.

Other methods of curving a stubborn branch are by steaming or soaking it in hot water. If the branch is steamed, the leaves and blossoms require protection during the process. You can cover them with newspaper. The branch must be tied in shape until it cools—preferably overnight. (Diagram II-B.)

The tallest branch (Shin) curves toward the back left- or right-hand corner of the container. Many schools call for keeping the bow of Shin (as well as the tip of Tai) within the outside dimension of the container. In other words, a narrow cylindrical container would require a fairly straight "formal" design while a usubata (with a broad top or curving sides) could be used for a less formal, sweeping arrangement. (Diagrams I-B and I-C.)

Auxiliary branches, shown in diagram I-B (center), give three levels of plant material, shaped more or less like a slender, gracefully pointed fan, with the highest (Shin) rib in the center and the lowest one nearest the arranger.

All lines behind the main branch are said to have a northern exposure, while those in front grow on the south. (Diagram I-A.) These branches are, therefore, like the thin and heavy lines in a drawing. In both the Shin and Soe (second-highest) groups the branch behind the main central branch should be longer and sparser than the front branch, to increase the illusion of depth.

The ratio, or proportionate length, established by the first Shin auxiliary branch should be maintained throughout the entire composition. In other words, if the second-tallest branch in the Shin group is three inches shorter than the first, the third branch in this group should in turn be three inches shorter than the second-tallest. This formula should be followed in both the Soe and Tai (lowest) groups in the arrangement.

The three groups, Shin, Soe, and Tai (or any one of them), may be full enough not to need strengthening, or they may incorporate additional lines which can either be coaxed or trimmed to serve as auxiliaries. For the sake of clarity each group in drawings throughout this book is made up of three lines; however, any number of auxiliaries may be added to strengthen any of these lines. It is necessary only that the three groups retain their separate identities, or prescribed shapes, and that all lines in the completed design be of different heights.

5. *Soe* (*man*).

This is the second-tallest line (or group) of the arrangement. In order to make this curve correspond to the Shin curve, bend the branch slightly about five inches below center (approximately one-seventh the distance between the tip and the mouth of the container); and then, two-thirds of the distance from the first bend to the tip, bend it back in the opposite direction. Soe follows Shin for about a quarter of Shin's height before sweeping out into a more generous curve (which extends some distance beyond Shin when viewed from above). Foliage and flowers should be on the upper side of this branch, facing Shin. (Diagram I-B.)

[24]

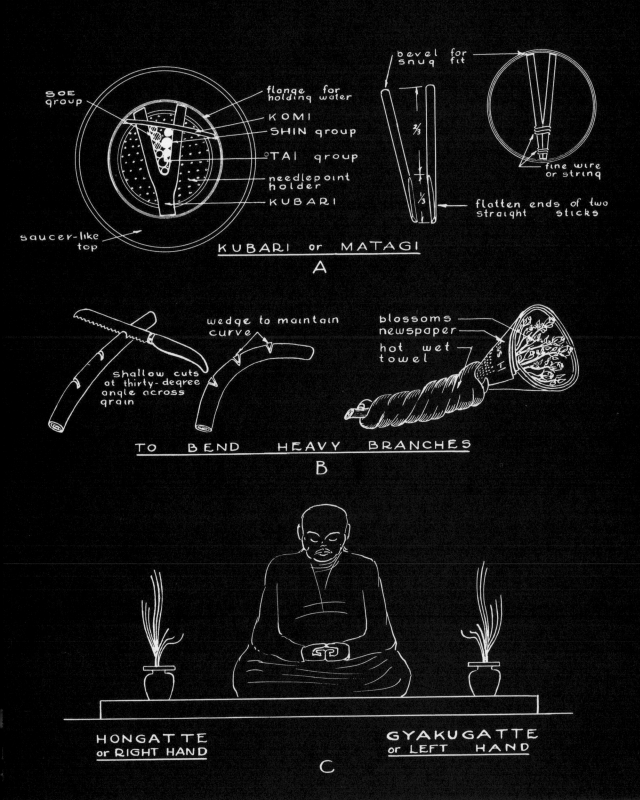

SOE group

flange for holding water

KOMI

SHIN group

TAI group

needlepoint holder

KUBARI

saucer-like top

bevel for snug fit

²⁄₃

¹⁄₃

fine wire or string

flatten ends of two straight sticks

KUBARI or MATAGI
A

shallow cuts at thirty-degree angle across grain

wedge to maintain curve

blossoms

newspaper

hot wet towel

TO BEND HEAVY BRANCHES
B

HONGATTE or RIGHT HAND

GYAKUGATTE or LEFT HAND

C

DIAGRAM II

Auxiliary branches follow the same general pattern as those in the Shin group—with three levels of plant material of correspondingly proportionate lengths. The group should be shaped more or less like a gracefully curved, elongated, concave, semi-circular fan, with the Soe rib pointing between the side and back of the container, the first supporting rib reaching well toward the back of the container, and the second auxiliary swinging in toward the front, nearer the Shin group. (Diagrams I-A and I-B.)

Nothing should be allowed to droop below the main line of this group and spoil its clarity.

6. *Tai (earth)*.

This is the lowest group of the arrangement. After following the same direction as the other two groups for about two inches (or slightly *below* the point where Soe leaves Shin) the line bends to the right (or in the opposite direction from other groups) at a much sharper angle. At two-thirds the distance from the first bend to the tip, the branch should be bent back, so that the tip rises sharply.

Although many schools require that the tip of the earth or Tai line stay within an imaginary line drawn vertically upward from the broadest part of the container (diagram I-C), the whole group should reach well toward the front of the container, pointing over the arranger's right or left shoulder, with all the tips looking up to the heaven or Shin line.

Auxiliary lines are governed by the same general principle of proportionate length as that of the two other groups, except that the branches should form an inverted triangle with the *shortest line in the center.* The branches might be likened to a convex fan with a crescent-shaped top, the exaggeratedly curved Tai rib pointing over the arranger's shoulder, the first auxiliary rib following the curve of the Shin group, and the second auxiliary (in the center) also conforming to the curve of Shin, but bowed out toward the front and looking up at Shin. Diagrams I-A and I-B demonstrate this point.

The entire Tai group is considered as having a southern exposure; therefore branches are more fully leafed and carry more blooms than the other two groups. The lowest placement of this group (the second auxiliary) usually shows the heaviest bloom, or fullest feeling of the entire arrangement.

Nothing should be allowed to droop below the main Tai line and detract from its graceful curve.

7. *Nemoto*.

This is the root or trunk of the "tree"—before the three main lines diverge; it is usually around four inches in height. However, it may vary from two inches to eight, depending upon the growing habit of the plant and the time of year. Trees naturally grow taller as the season advances. (Diagram I-B.)

In order to obtain a smooth, closely related trunk or nemoto, all rough places and foliage should be removed from the lower half of the Shin branch or branches, from the lower third of the Soe group, and from approximately half of the Tai group.

The smoother and straighter this part of each stem is, the closer together all of them will fit in the holder and the more unified and "trunklike" they will appear in

[26]

the arrangement. Upon this close union at the base depends the strength of the individual lines as well as the visual balance of the design as a whole.

The nemoto is a practical aid in prolonging the life of plant material. It not only prevents decaying leaves from contaminating the water and exposes maximum stem surface for water absorption, but also cuts down on the amount of foliage requiring moisture.

8. *Nejime*.

This "root-hider" of flowers may replace the Tai group if needed to avoid a "feeling of loneliness" where stems emerge from the container. The nejime should follow the same general proportions and shape as the group it is replacing.

The Japanese do not use another kind of tree, or blooming trees with different flowers, for this purpose. Most schools *require* a nejime with pine, juniper, or other non-flowering branches, but list only a few exceptions where blossoms may be used with a flowering tree or shrub.

9. *Simplest order for inserting stems in kubari.*

(a) See diagram II-A. Force the main Tai line firmly into the crotch of the Y; follow with the second auxiliary and end with the first auxiliary stem.

(b) Start with the second auxiliary stem of Shin, follow with Shin, and end with the first auxiliary stem.

(c) Start with Soe's second auxiliary stem, follow with the main Soe stem, and end with the first auxiliary stem.

When using a kubari without the aid of a supplemental needlepoint holder, form a V over the crotch of the Y with the thumb and forefinger of the left hand. Place the material in the container with your right hand and pull each placement firmly into the crotch with the forefinger of your left hand while holding the ends of the previously placed stems against the crotch of the Y with your remaining fingers *underneath* the kubari. The position of your left hand should not be changed until all the stems have been placed and are properly braced in the crotch by the komi (the small stick described on page 24 and shown in diagram II-A).

With some types of sweeping material a more graceful effect may be achieved by following the method of the Enshiu school, which places the Soe group in front of Shin and the Tai group behind it.

Regardless of which procedure is followed, Shin should stand firmly in the center of the design. Although it should appear to be standing upright and facing Soe, it may be turned slightly toward the arranger (to present the best profile). If necessary to balance the forward movement of Tai, the Shin line may also lean a little toward the back of the container. The best foliage on Shin should be in front and toward the southwest, with the east side of the branch or stems stripped almost bare. (The inner side of the Shin bow lies on the "In" or "shady" side with most of the flowers and foliage facing southwest and front.) The backs of flowers are seldom shown (except when specially used that way to point a moral), but blossoms and foliage are used in profile to expose both sides in different proportion.

[27]

10. *Final check*.

Photographs sometimes create the illusion that Ikenobo arrangements are flat, this is not so; or at least it should not be so. The tips of Shin, Soe, and Tai should lie diagonally across the container from back to front with Tai pointing over the viewer's left or right shoulder. (Diagram I-A.) They should not be in a straight line from left to right. Every effort should be made to avoid the appearance of flatness. As in painting or sculpture, the design is intended primarily to be looked at directly from the front; however, as in those arts, the effect from the sides is also considered.

(a) Make sure that the nemoto is neat and firmly held together, with Soe leaving Shin a little above the point where Tai swings away from the main line, and that the tip of Shin is immediately over the point where the nemoto leaves the water. (Diagram I-B.)

(b) Check to be certain that the three groups are clearly defined and that no two lines in the composition are of identical height.

(c) Remove drooping foliage, flowers, and twigs, as well as those that interfere with the clean-cut lines and sharp angles of the arrangement. (A dampened finger dipped into dirt or ashes will cover scars left by trimming.)

(d) All lines should face Shin with tips, blossoms, and foliage carefully turned upward so they may "catch the dew."

Left: Japanese-style flower arrangements can never grow monotonous for, no matter how closely the rules or classic patterns are followed, variety is always achieved through the individuality of the plant material itself. Each flower has a distinct personality which makes it impossible to recreate a design exactly, even with carefully selected, apparently identical material.

Note in this arrangement how the largest flower has been placed at the bottom and the smallest, half-open one at the top—a rule customarily followed by Occidental arrangers. (Photos: *Photographic Arts.*)

Right: Here we see the same group of roses transferred to a different container. Simply by lifting the flowers (intact in their needlepoint holder) out of the tall vase, and placing them in this round black pottery bowl, a completely new effect has been achieved.

The design no longer has a strong vertical feeling, but the large leaves placed at the lower right-hand side again act as a counterbalance for the heavy left-hand placement of flowers.

A third and entirely new over-all design was created by lifting the same rose design bodily out of the round vase and placing it in this shallow container.

Here the visual weight of the exposed portion of the container counterbalances the weight of the flowers placed at the extreme left, while black lava rocks conceal the needle-point holder and give an interesting textural contrast.

Japanese principles were again adapted in making this arrangement in an antique bronze usubata.

One side of this design shows bronze magnolia leaves arranged in the three Ikenobo levels. The coral anthurium leads the eye down into a graceful group of chili peppers which are slightly lighter in hue. (Photos: Anthony Stoker.)

The Ikenobo rules concerning depth and proportion have been used in this arrangement; otherwise it departs from Japanese tradition. A dramatic effect is achieved by making a single vertical design in a pair of alabaster urns. The three-dimensional composition, created for an important position in a Georgian drawing room, is a time-saver as well as an eye-catcher.

The vertical shaft of pampas grass at the rear of the design, together with the forward curving thrust of the grapes, forms a permanent background against which fresh roses or other flowers can be substituted as the older blossoms fade. Gladioli, carnations, spider chrysanthemums, or any suitable seasonal material can take their place without disturbing the design in any way. An elegant year-round composition is thus assured with the change of only a few flowers. (Photo: *Photographic Arts.*)

The other side of the arrangement on page 31 makes
special use of the top, saucer-shaped portion of the usubata.
The glycerine-treated magnolia is again apparent, but Hubbard
squash and clusters of pecans replace the anthurium. The group
of peppers makes an effective transition of color in the design.

II: NAGEIRE

Informal Arrangements

Nageire or "throw-in" arrangements, were the first recorded home designs and yet, according to legend, they were born on a battlefield!

It was a hot summer's day in the year 1592, and by mutual agreement the two armies engaged in bitter conflict over the subjugation of Adonora paused so that their generals might enjoy a quiet cup of tea. General Hideyoshi had (in a primitive effort at air conditioning) ordered the lacquered bucket used for his pampered charger to be filled with water and placed before him. His favorite tea master was officiating and, in war or peace, he liked to serve tea in the accepted manner. A flower arrangement was required to help create the correct spiritual atmosphere. He looked about him, then plucked an iris from the river, grouped a few leaves around it, drew the dagger carried in the sheath of his sword, pierced the stems with its blade, and tossed the group into the beautiful black bucket before the general. The iris swayed uncertainly for a moment on its slender stem, then came to rest with the bloom slanting welcomingly toward General Hideyoshi and the leaves assuming a graceful natural pose.

"How cleverly your 'throw-in' took position!" exclaimed the general, delighted with his tea master's resourcefulness. From that day on Nageire, or flowers apparently carelessly tossed into a container, grew in popularity as a part of the tea ceremony.

So much stress was placed on the skill of the arranger in Ikenobo designs that some students felt that interpretation of the plant material was being overshadowed. The "throw-in" school claimed to express nature more realistically. The beauty of the graceful designs called for projecting even the personality of climbing and leaning plants in an apparently normal, unrestrained manner. Most plants were treated by the leaning method (as much in deference to the ingenuity of the long-ago tea master as because his followers claimed that most plants lean).

The stems rested against the back of the vase and slanted across the container, leaning forward in a free, unstudied manner. Unlike that of the older classic designs, beauty of line here was, if necessary, subordinated to better express the nature of the flowers, and stems were no longer uncompromisingly forced into the attitude of a single shrub or tree.

It was a free and flexible adaptation of the classic style. The sparse lines were devoid of many attributes, giving a pure feeling of form—a studied artlessness—which emphasized the beauty of the individual flower. Although a single tree could still be interpreted, flowers now predominated and for the first time there was a feeling of color spilling over and softening the lip of the container.

However, as time passed the pendulum swung so far that these "free" designs became rather stiff modifications in casual balance. The extensions were balanced by heavier flowers, much as the architect or bridge builder employs the cantilever principle, and although they fulfilled the requirement of suggesting nature they lacked the ordered symbolism so necessary to the people.

During the seventeenth and eighteenth centuries, interest in the arrangement of plant material spread to all classes. The momentum increased with the daily usage of flowers in the home and waves of new meaning, as well as varied forms, swept the country. Many different schools sprang up. Some grew and flourished; others, lacking true significance, were soon forgotten.

No longer could flower arranging be termed a leisure-time diversion of priests and warriors. It was now a social requirement for anyone with the slightest pretense of culture.

Although the Ikenobo Shin, Soe, and Tai are used for designating elemental branches throughout this book, much philosophical thinking went into the names given to various levels of material, and this is only a minor indication of the profound ideas underlying the art. Man is usually shown standing between heavenly aspirations (meditation) and earthly activity. Although he never actually overshadows heaven, in some schools he may soar above heaven or trail below earth, but always he unifies and reflects the conception of life as a continual ceremony.

Typical of the thinking behind the various schools was the change of the heaven, or central, branch, to Tai, the body or substance of all things; So (with a slightly different spelling and meaning) became aspect or phenomenon; and the lowest branch, Yu, stood for activity or the working of all things. Tai (the main branch) in this school includes earth, water, fire, wind, and air, as well as the mind common to both animate and inanimate objects. So originates all virtues, which show forth brilliantly transformed into Yu, or exquisite activity—the harmonizer of man and nature, spirit and matter. Thus again the three greatnesses permeating the universe were gracefully clothed and tangibly presented in slightly different form through the "way of flowers."

By the end of the eighteenth century Nageire designs had taken their present triangular form. As in Ikenobo, each group was triangular and complete in itself, yet each was an essential part of the whole greater triangle. The primary difference lay in balance, or deviation from the ideal shape worked out by the Ikenobo priests. However, natural beauty was still used to symbolize the harmony between spiritual truth and material substance.

[36]

The new Nageire originated in the *bunzin* (literati) school of Japanese painting and was bunzin-like in its conception. It brought great variety and gaiety to the art. The old school had been influenced by the tea ceremony, and its arrangements, though simple, were somewhat methodical, even somber, in character. The new Nageire accepted the past forms plus some added elements. Though devoted to projecting plant "personality" in an apparently artless way, it recognized that all flowers and branches have some superfluous parts. This meant that for the first time bushy or leafy plants were considered suitable for floral designs.

The designs often consisted of only one well-shaped branch with a few sprays of flowers at its base, the woody branch representing the "male" and the flowers the "female" principle. However, each "originator" made his own rules and endeavored to gain followers for his particular method. Most schools prescribed one "attractive" branch supplemented by a shorter one (placed somewhat higher or lower) with its base hugging the main branch to indicate that they sprang from one point. A few flowers were usually added for Tai or, with blossoming branches, a third fuller branch might be substituted. The tips of these three placements formed a triangle (rather than the diagonal line created by Ikenobo placements) and an uneven number of flowers was in some schools not mandatory.

The freedom of the new design lent itself to less formal and expensive containers; thus even those who were not fortunate enough to possess handsome bronzes and elegant porcelains could bring the outdoor world into their homes. With an informal design in a simple tall container they could adapt the old rules and proportions to their own tastes, as well as to their more humble dwellings.

Nageire arrangements (made for special occasions in the home or tea houses) were to be viewed politely by the guest of honor only when seated on a mat directly in front of the *tokonoma,* or alcove (see page 134), and they were sometimes a bit "lonesome-looking" on one side. They were usually placed against one wall of the tokonoma with the lower line reaching toward the other side as if seeking light or pointing toward the garden. As in Ikenobo designs, they were considered master, man, or right-hand arrangements if the Tai or earth line reached toward the right, and left-hand (guest or female) arrangements if it reached toward the left—a carry-over from the old *rikkwa* temple designs customarily placed on the right and left side of Buddha. (Diagram II-C on page 27.)

Nageire designs were much simpler to make than the classic types, and since they were not religious offerings the fleeting quality of the material was no longer of prime importance. In the home a guest might be honored by an arrangement symbolizing the mystery of nature and the universe, even though the flowers lasted only until the guest departed or the ceremony was completed.

Japanese sages are fond of pointing out that naturalness is the font of life, the source of true beauty. They claim that a peaceful generation may idly seek beauty in artificiality, but that those born in an age of turmoil and war, forced to face harsh reality, find special satisfaction only in recreating the unstudied informality of nature herself.

A leaning Nageire-style design featuring blue juniper, lemon-yellow freesia, and a dragon-shaped piece of weathered wood.

The elegant burl used under the container (a bronze ritual vase) balances the forward movement of the design and repeats the coloring and texture of the mahogany desk on which the arrangement is placed.

The juniper and the weathered wood (*boku*) functions as a permanent background; the freesia can be replaced with fresh blooms or other flowers as occasion and availability of material dictate. Juniper can be made "long lasting" by adding glycerine to the water in the container (one part glycerine to two parts water) when the design is first made. The juniper takes on attractive shades of golden brown as it absorbs the glycerine, and old pieces of wood like the one used here, also mellow interestingly during the same process.

Juniper and cypress are considered the most ancient of trees; both are highly favored in Shinto and Buddhist ceremonial arrangements. (Photo: John Hugelmeyer.)

A single pine branch frames a few apparently casually placed zinnias in this adaptation of a Nageire design. Each cluster of pine needles was trimmed to decrease its apparent size and coaxed to look upward. The container was placed on a waxed oak block to give added visual weight at the base of the design. The bright yellow flowers pick up coloring in the room and emphasize both the color and rough texture of the pottery container.

Many varieties of pine grow in Japan, and the variously formed, long-lasting branches are commonly used in all types of arrangements. Some trunks and branches are strong and massive, some curve gracefully and appear very elegant, some are uniform in shape, and some cling to rocky ledges and look tortured and windswept. The age of any tree makes a difference both in form and coloring. Young trees have branches with soft, fresh needles of lighter coloring, and buds or cones vary with the season.

The Japanese choose different varieties of pine to express certain meanings. Trees bearing five needles to a group are preferred for congratulatory and auspicious occasions, while those that grow in pairs are used at weddings. (When one withers and dies the other drops also.) (Photo: Lawrence Joseph.)

[40]

Two branches of nandina are combined with three coral-colored anthurium blossoms and three leaves. The color scheme, including the chartreuse container, was chosen to harmonize with the furnishings of the dining room. The walls are soft green and the chairs (not shown in the photo) are upholstered in a two-tone coral fabric. The tall container and tall lines of the Nageire-style design emphasize the vertical bars of the room divider, a portion of which is seen at left.

Anthurium is an expensive flower, but it is a practical choice, since the blossoms remain fresh for several weeks. Nandina, too, lasts a long time if it is properly conditioned. (Photo: Gottscho-Schleisner, Inc.)

Two soaring, pale-green, unopened palmetto fronds form the height of this arrangement. And grouped below them are clusters of black carrion berries, three crimson double hibiscus, and a few bronze-colored galax leaves. The black teak stand used under the brass container repeats the color of the berries and sets off the design.

Except for the hibiscus the arrangement could easily be turned into a permanent one. Palmetto eventually dries to an attractive soft gray-green and the carrion berries and galax leaves retain most of their original color. Instead of the hibiscus hemerocallis, glamellias, camellias, or even carnations could be used for an equally attractive effect.

Containers with broad necks and open expanses of water are popular with Japanese arrangers, since flowers last longer in receptacles which allow free passage of air. However, in this design none of the material actually requires water. Hibiscus lives only for a day either in or out of water. (Photo: Lawrence Joseph.)

Construction Details for Making Nageire Arrangements

1. *Selecting the three main lines.*

The three main lines of a Nageire design may be cut to the same proportions as those prescribed for an Ikenobo arrangement (diagram I), or the length of stems may differ radically. The choice will largely depend upon the location, the type of container, and the natural growing habit of the material. The Soe line may curve gracefully up to two or even three times the height of Shin, or it may flow downward until it all but reaches the floor. A Nageire design has few limitations, yet it must be remembered that the strength of any good arrangement rests on a well-established central axis and that the Shin line, regardless of its length, should be the hub of the design with all other lines centering around it.

The branch or flowering stem with the most vigorous-looking tip should be selected for the Shin line and then put aside until you determine whether it is to be the longest, as well as the central, line.

If a more interesting but less vigorous branch or stem is available which conforms to the plant's erect, flowing, or trailing growing habit, it should be set aside for the Soe line.

After deciding upon what position the Shin and Soe lines will take in the design, select Tai and cut it to an appropriate length to balance the design. Should Soe be a flowing or trailing line, a more compact, somewhat foreshortened Tai will usually prove the best choice, and vice versa.

2. *Cutting the three main lines.*

(a) If Shin is to be the longest line, follow the directions given for the Ikenobo arrangement in Chapter I.

(b) If Soe is to be the longest line, establish its length and angle first (considering the natural growing habit of the material, the container, and the location for which the arrangement is intended). Hold the branch against the container at the most effective angle and cut it to the required length. (Diagram III-A.) It is better not to let a line flow more than two-thirds the distance from the lip of the container to the floor. A longer line is apt to overpower the design and will prove very difficult to balance.

(c) Cut Shin from one-third to two-thirds the height of Soe; then cut Tai from one-third to two-thirds the height of Shin, selecting the most suitable lengths in proportion to the size of the container. If in doubt, it is better to cut the stems a little longer than necessary, for it is easy to shorten them later.

All measurements should allow ample length to compensate for the portions of the stems which will be inside the container.

Longest lines should always be cut first. When adding strengthening or auxiliary lines, bear in mind that keeping from one-half to two-thirds of the mouth of the container free of plant material will lead to the most pleasing, uncluttered designs. (Diagrams III-B and III-D.)

[46]

3. *Holding the branches in place.*

Japanese arrangers seldom use holders for this type of design; however, the simplest process in any fairly broad-mouthed, tall container is to fill the container two-thirds full of bird gravel and place a heavy needlepoint holder on top of it. (Diagram III-A.) The holder may be fixed permanently in place by pouring paraffin on top of the gravel and bedding the holder in paraffin while it is still warm.

If flowing branches will not remain in position when attached to the holder, they can be controlled as indicated in diagram III-C.

The addition of a kubari will also prove helpful with certain designs and materials.

4. *Shin.*

Even in apparently casual arrangements the Japanese achieve a pleasing balance by placing the Shin line so that the tip of it is above the point where the stem leaves the container. If a branch is not quite correctly shaped to assume this position, it can be bent. The general rule to follow (outlined in Chapter I) is to bend the branch at a point halfway between the tip and mouth of the container, and then, at about a two-thirds distance from the tip to the first bend, force it back in the opposite direction.

Auxiliary branches in this main group should be added as heretofore to form the shape of a pointed fan, with Shin in the center. The first supporting branch, the sparsest and longest (#1) should be placed in the back, and the second, shorter auxiliary branch (#2) should be arranged in front, as in diagram III-D. (If the first auxiliary branch is three inches shorter than Shin, then the second one should be made three inches shorter still.)

For the sake of clarity in the drawings, groups of branches are made up of three separate lines; however, fewer auxiliaries may be needed and any number of auxiliaries may be added to strengthen Shin, Soe, or Tai, as long as groups retain the prescribed shapes and no lines in the finished composition appear to be of identical length. (Diagram III-D.)

5. *Soe.*

Regardless of the length of Soe, a pleasing line can always be obtained by bending the branch in the manner previously described. The first bend should be made a few inches above the mouth of the container.

Auxiliary branches should be added so that you have three proportionate levels of material. The longer the Soe branch, the greater the difference should be between its length and the length of its auxiliary branches. In other words, the first auxiliary branch for a three-foot Soe might be from five to seven inches shorter than Soe and the second auxiliary branch from five to seven inches shorter than that. A two-foot Soe might call for a difference of three to four inches in the length of each of the auxiliaries.

No matter what the length or position of Soe, the group should be shaped like a concave semi-circular fan, with the Soe rib pointing toward the side and front of the container (or trailing down over it), the first supporting rib following the direction of Soe and reaching slightly more toward the back, and the second supporting rib following the direction of the other two lines but curving in a little more toward the Shin group.

[47]

Tips of *all* branches should reach toward Shin: nothing should droop below Soe and spoil its clarity. No matter whether Soe is erect, flowing, or trailing, it represents the boundary line of the arrangement and all auxiliaries should be placed between this and the Shin line.

6. *Tai.*

Here again, regardless of length, the Tai line can be given pleasing curves by bending the branch in the manner prescribed for Shin and Soe. Make the first bend slightly lower on the stem than the one in the Soe branch, then curve it the other way, two-thirds of the distance from this bend to the tip of the branch.

It is usually necessary to shorten and thicken the entire Tai group to compensate for a flowing or trailing Soe line. However, where Soe is taller than Shin, a slender, flowing Tai group, somewhat exaggerated in length, will usually make a better design.

Auxiliary branches for this group allow considerable leeway, and their length and placement will depend upon the visual weight of the material and the height of the other groups.

The first auxiliary stem should follow the Shin line rather closely; it may be one-half the length of Shin or even the same length as Tai if this provides a more effective balance for the other two groups.

The second auxiliary branch may vary from one inch less than Tai to three-fourths the length of the first auxiliary, regardless of the difference between Tai and Tai's first auxiliary.

No matter what length of line is established, the Tai group should form the shape of a convex fan with a crescent top, as shown in diagram III-D.

It will help in trying to visualize this group to remember that while the longest rib in both Shin and Soe groups is the main or central line, the center line of Tai is the *shortest*—the second auxiliary to Tai.

7. *Nemoto.*

A clearly defined "root" or base is not essential in this free design, and in some instances the material may even rest on the lip of the container. However, all lines should be closely united where they leave the container, and the design will usually prove more satisfactory if these lines hold together for an inch or two before separating.

A kubari will prove helpful in achieving this effect. Place the kubari one-half inch below the surface of the water with the single end of the Y pointing toward the spot where the line of the longest branch will cross the lip of the container—in other words toward Soe or Tai, whichever is longer.

In every type of design all rough places and foliage should be removed from the portion of stems which come into contact with water. This not only provides a compact "root" but prolongs the life of the material.

8. *Nejime.*

A "root-hider" made up of flowers usually serves as the Tai group in informal designs. Nageire arrangements frequently have Shin and Soe groups made with one kind of flower, while Tai is another color or an entirely different type of bloom. In this

[48]

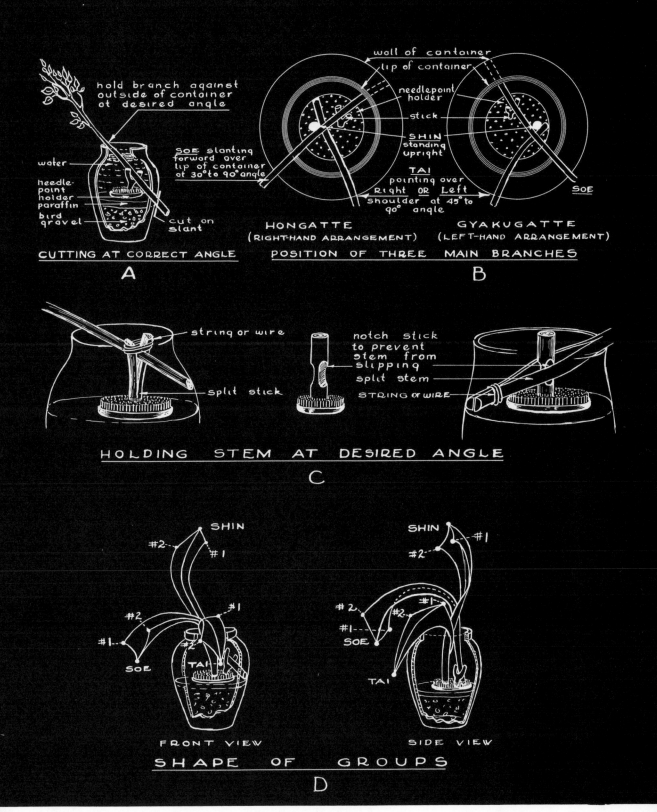

A

hold branch against
outside of container
at desired angle

water
heedle-
point
holder
paraffin
bird
gravel

cut on
slant

SOE slanting
forward over
lip of container
at 30° to 90° angle

CUTTING AT CORRECT ANGLE

B

woll of container
lip of container
needlepoint
holder
stick
SHIN
standing
upright

TAI
pointing over
Right OR Left
shoulder at 45° to
90° angle

SOE

HONGATTE
(RIGHT-HAND ARRANGEMENT)

GYAKUGATTE
(LEFT-HAND ARRANGEMENT)

POSITION OF THREE MAIN BRANCHES

C

string or wire

split stick

notch stick
to prevent
stem from
slipping
split stem
STRING or WIRE

HOLDING STEM AT DESIRED ANGLE

D

SHIN
#2
#1

#2
#1
#1
SOE
TAI

FRONT VIEW

SHIN
#1
#2

#2
#1
#1
SOE

TAI

SIDE VIEW

SHAPE OF GROUPS

DIAGRAM III

school a different type of bloom is now permitted with flowering branches, and some schools allow an even number of flowers.

9. *Simplest order for inserting stems in holder.*

(a) If the longest line is Shin, follow instructions for Ikenobo.

(b) If a kubari is used and the longest line is not Shin, establish the longest line and auxiliaries firmly in the crotch of the Y; follow with Tai (or Soe, whichever is longer) and end up by placing the Shin group.

(c) When not using a kubari, establish the longest line first regardless of what group it belongs to, follow with Shin and its first and second auxiliaries, then place the first and second auxiliaries of the longest line; end with either Tai or Soe (whichever is shorter) and its two auxiliaries.

Shin should always stand firmly in the center of the design with its best side facing front. Soe may either stand at a thirty-degree angle from Shin or flow gracefully toward the side-front of the vase. Tai, balancing the group, should lean away from Shin at a forty-five-degree angle, reaching out toward the arranger's right or left shoulder, or trailing down over the center and front of the container.

All lines, regardless of their length or position in the design, should face toward Shin, while Shin faces side and front (toward Soe) and the arranger.

10. *Final check.*

(a) See that the tips of Shin, Soe, and Tai form the points of a triangle.

(b) All stems should lead out of the container together and toward one side of it.

(c) The tip of Shin should be positioned approximately over the point where the stem emerges from the water. (Diagrams III-B and III-D.)

(d) Check the shape of the three main groups for clarity of line and make sure that no two lines in the composition are of the same height.

(e) No drooping foliage or flowers should be present.

(f) Check the arrangement for depth. If the design appears to be toppling forward, add necessary material behind the Shin group. It is better to put several sparse lines, or buds, in this position rather than one heavy line, or fully opened flower, since this is a "northern exposure." The added material should lean slightly backward, with tip (or tips) showing somewhere between Tai auxiliaries #1 and #2.

(g) All groups should face or compliment Shin. The tips of the branches, the flowers, and the fronts of all leaves (glossy or sunny side) should look up toward the sun as they would if actually growing.

III: **MORIBANA**

Garden Scenes

M*oribana* designs, which made their appearance in the early part of the twentieth century, seemed like a complete departure from any previous Japanese school. Instead of depicting one aspect of nature, Moribana arrangements represented nature more fully; they suggested not only an individual plant or line of growth but also the surroundings and growing conditions of the material used. They were, in essence, stylized arrangements inspired by familiar Japanese landscape and garden scenes.

But in spite of this "new look," the lines of the separate groups and of the composition as a whole followed quite closely the tridimensional pattern set by the earlier schools. Moribana was a happy blend of Nageire and Ikenobo; one might say that it expressed natural scenery through a free Nageire interpretation of Ikenobo curves and proportions. Although the arrangements were sometimes made up of widely separated groups and were not confined to any definition of form, the proportion of the material adhered closely to the old rules.

The word *mori*, meaning "heaped up" or "profuse," affixed to *bana*, meaning "flowers," is rather deceptive to the Occidental. For although Moribana designs often incorporate two or more separate groupings of plant material, approximately one-half the surface of the water is left free. The flowers are not heaped up or profuse as we are accustomed to see them in European arrangements, let alone in old Dutch still lifes. But it must be remembered that the design was named by the Japanese who were accustomed to seeing a *single* well-defined root in all their floral compositions. So the "new look" appeared "heaped up" to them.

The scenic arrangements were made in large traylike containers. Great leeway was allowed in mechanical aids as well as in the choice of material and the form in which it was arranged. Any combination was acceptable—provided the plants were arranged according to their nature: trees or mountainous material were placed high in the design, grasses and water plants were placed lower, and so on. The old taboos against

Ligustrum, pink water lilies, and two pieces of gnarled wood were used to suggest a vigorous, wind-tortured tree leaning over a peaceful pond. The cliff-viewing, double-rooted Moribana design is arranged in a soft gray wood container made waterproof by a metal lining.

Arrangements like this will grace the table of any dining room; however, a formal setting would require a smooth-textured container. Needlepoint holders are easily concealed by leaves or driftwood. (Photo: *Photographic Arts.*)

thorny or food plants were discarded, and even the prohibitions about using evil-smelling plants or material that was poisonous in any of its parts were often ignored. Nevertheless, hothouse flowers were not combined with yard-grown or roadside material, and the use of out-of-season specimens was considered in poor taste except when it signified the expected or hoped-for return of an honored guest at a time when the flower would naturally be in bloom. Flowers past their prime or past their season were called "dead flowers," and to use them was considered a breach of etiquette.

To make the interpretation of a landscape convincing, the plants selected were arranged in their normal growing positions. If mountain pine was combined with flowers found growing at the seashore, the pine was naturally arranged to stand much higher than the flowers. In other details too the scene would suggest a specific locale with harmonious groups of "friendly" plants "growing" together in compatible surroundings.

No woodland scene or garden was complete without some suggestion of water. The groups could be placed at opposite corners of the large container, leaving a "fish way" of water between; or a branch might reach across the container to create a "water-viewing" or "cliff-viewing" design.

Kansuike or "water-viewing" arrangements derived their name from the Chinese and Japanese characters for "scenery"—literally reading "mountain and water." This type of design became very popular. In Japan a Kansuike arrangement is symbolically male (or right-handed) when the "weight" is placed on the right side of the container and it is female or pertains to a guest when the weight is arranged to fall on the left. Thus the type of the arrangement is not indicated by the placement of Tai, as in other designs.

People who have traveled through Japan will have observed that Japanese garden design is based on the conception of a natural landscape in miniature. In much the same way Moribana designs represent Japanese gardens in miniature. In both instances topographical features are symbolized by plant material. This suggestion is usually very subtle: mountains can be represented by pines and fern, rocks and stones by pine branches, plains by wild flowers and grasses, lakes and rivers by white chrysanthemums or water plants. (The water of the sea, however, is left to the viewer's imagination.)

Neither Japanese gardens nor Moribana arrangements are made up of geometric patterns, although such designs are apt to come into the Occidental mind when a landscape garden is spoken of. Balance in both instances is achieved through the relationship of fluid lines and swelling curves, not through symmetrically spaced area relationship. The art of placing even a single growing plant within the confines of a vase closely follows the principles of Japanese garden design. Many great flower masters were in fact also renowned as landscape architects.

The first master of Ikenobo incorporated water in his original "Hermitage by the Lake," and such was his influence on the art of gardening that even today a Japanese garden without water or the suggestion of water (often represented by sand or water-worn rocks) is unthinkable.

The proportion of exposed water in the large round or oblong containers used for most Moribana designs was made to vary with the season; however, regardless of the

[54]

time of year, some water was usually visible. All schools are influenced by the changing seasons, but Moribana lays particular stress on this phase, for the designs are inspired by nature's many moods. In spring, the lines are made to rise from the central section of the container in vigorous sweeping curves that suggest new growth. In summer, the weight of material (voluptuously full) is shown toward the back of the container, spreading above broad expanses of exposed water. Winter arrangements are placed near the front of the container; the material often appears dormant, with heavy moss covering most of the water.

In Moribana, as in other types of arrangements, flower masters attain perfection with as little material as possible. Lakes, distant mountains, hills, and plains are all suggested by the clever arrangement of a few plant cuttings in the shallow receptacle.

Materials that might not in themselves seem distinctive are often used to represent certain natural elements in a design and to evoke certain memories. However, actual growth found in a particular outdoor setting need not be used to interpret it in miniature, any more than a specific tree need be copied faithfully in an Ikenobo arrangement. Trees or complete scenes are usually *suggested* in an idealized composite form. In other words, the artist uses branches, foliage, and flowers to re-create a natural scene stylistically. He also uses such material to suggest some particular season or spiritual aspect.

Although Ikenobo and Nageire designs give a satisfying feeling of depth when viewed from the front, Moribana arrangements present a three-dimensional quality regardless of the side from which they are viewed. (This makes them especially useful for dining- or coffee-table arrangements in the Occidental home.)

As in classic designs, every effort was made to stress a feeling of growth. The *kenzin*, literally "sword mountain" or "nails standing up" (parent of our needlepoint holder), was never covered with material that would appear to lie lifelessly on the water. All material was arranged as if growing, both to express growth and to keep the water clean. Pebbles were used to cover the kenzin in arrangements of water plants, but instead of being piled in flat, meaningless mounds, they were grouped to form graceful curves as if they had been washed up on the river's edge or the shore of a lake.

Boku sticks or gnarled pieces of wood (predecessors of our driftwood), as well as weathered stones, suggested the earthy source of flowers and provided natural contrasts in shape and texture.

An entire chapter could be devoted to the use of stones alone (which were enjoyed "by arranging fashionably"). They balanced heavy branches, lent strength and dignity to slender grasses, and emphasized the beauty of delicate wild flowers. White stones were reserved for summer, red for fall, black for winter, and green for spring; each had a definite place and individual meaning in the design.

The success of a Moribana arrangement hinges as much upon knowing where to put the emphasis as upon the design itself. By selecting the significant elements in the scene and in the plant material a specific scene is evoked in the spectator's mind. It is transmitted by symbol and idea with no attempt at complete representation. Some plants attract attention primarily by their conspicuous blooms, such as the Easter lily and peony, some by the grace of their branches, such as pine and plum, and some by the individuality of their foliage, such as the iris and water lily. Each of these plants shows to best advantage when its most characteristic feature is emphasized. For instance, a bunch of iris blooms will represent little more than an indeterminate mass of color, but should one or two iris be used discriminately with their swordlike leaves the beauty of each flower will stand out in sharp relief. Similarly, much of the ethereal beauty of plum blossoms will be lost if the flowers are massed instead of being considered as embellishments for an interestingly shaped branch.

Not knowing where to place the center of attention might be said to be as disastrous to an arrangement as allowing the bass in an opera to sing the part written for the soprano. To obtain the best results an arranger must be able not only to recognize the character, the inherent weakness or strength, of the material available to him, but also where and how to organize it for the most harmonious effect. He must know, furthermore, in what respects the particular scene he is depicting differs from other similar scenes, and how to express its characteristics through the material at hand.

The container plays an important part in Moribana arrangements. The Japanese use perfectly round, glaringly white bowls almost exclusively for practice work during lessons. Oblong white trays are sometimes used in early spring to suggest a snow-white field in miniature, but even in these designs a soft blue lining (the color of distant water) is preferred. Although it is true that white is conspicuous enough to tolerate more weight than softer colors, it is much safer to concentrate on colors which form nature's backgrounds. The soft browns or tans of rocks and earth, mottled grays and blues of sky and clouds, or the subdued shades of shadowy green water and moss-covered stones will prove more effective than an uncompromising white.

Even those who are interested only in the more obvious beauty presented through a Moribana arrangement will derive much pleasure from the seasonal changes which they express. Neither the most expensive painting nor a triumphantly perfect piece of sculpture can provide more satisfaction, beauty, or stimulation than a Moribana design correctly placed in the Occidental home.

Construction Details for Making Garden Scenes

1. *Selecting the three main lines.*
After studying available material and considering which container to use, four things should be decided:

(a) Which element to feature—branch, foliage, or bloom.

(b) Whether a single, double, or multiple-rooted design will best convey the idea.

(c) Whether the main body of the design would be most effective on the left or right side of the container. (The location of the arrangement will be the deciding factor.)

(d) Whether emphasis should fall toward the front or back of the container. (In a classic Moribana, emphasis on the central part of the container indicates spring and fall; front, winter; back, summer.)

If the location, container, and natural growing habit of the material call for a single-rooted design, the three main lines may be cut to the proportions set out for either Ikenobo or Nageire.

The length of Shin is usually determined by measuring the length and width of the shallow container. The maximum height in all Japanese arrangements is based on the growing habit as well as the visual weight of the container and material. (The taller the arrangement, the more drama it will have.)

Although the holder for Shin may be placed practically anywhere in the container, the design will usually prove more satisfactory if the weight is not concentrated too near the center or crowded against the edges of the container.

There is considerable leeway in form as well as in position of the design in the container. Several holders may be required—even for a design incorporating only one main line around which all others are grouped. However, at least half the surface of the water should be left free of plant material, and all groups (as well as the over-all design) should maintain a triangular, tridimensional outline.

Even in flat containers the most beautiful (and most popular) designs are usually those which depict a single tree with a few flowers growing at its feet.

A line with vigorous tip or strong bud should be selected for Shin, a flowing, graceful line for Soe, and appropriate flowers with self-foliage for Tai. (These flowers should be in scale, as well as culturally compatible with material used for Shin and Soe.)

2. *Cutting the three main lines.*

(a) Shin should be cut as long as the location, growing habit of the plant, and visual weight of the material and container will allow.

(b) For a water-viewing or cliff-viewing design Soe should reach gracefully across the water; its length usually approximates the length or else the diameter of the container. However, a Soe line extending beyond the rim of the container may be difficult to balance; its length, therefore, depends upon the placement of the design in the container. In a double-rooted design, the groups are usually placed to face each other diagonally across the container. To facilitate securing a heavy branch to the holder at an angle, first cut the branch to approximately the right length, then hold it in the water-filled container at the best angle and re-cut along the slant marked by the water line. (Diagram IV-A.)

(c) Tai should be from one-half to one-third the height of Shin, whichever is most compatible with the design and with the growing habit of the material.

Longest lines should always be cut first. When adding lines bear in mind that, although at least one-half of the surface of the water should be kept free of plant material, the design should be full enough to look pleasing from all sides.

If the design is to depict a lake shore in the foreground and mountains in the

[57]

background, make the foreground group small, full, and greatly foreshortened, and the background group compact and exaggerated in height. On the other hand, if the scene depicts mountains in the foreground and a lake shore in the distance, the small group should be sparse as well as foreshortened; thus depth, both real and implied, increases the illusion of distance.

There should be consistent proportion between the groups and the idea, as well as the container, location, and growing habit of material.

Where the groups are set far apart to represent a garden scene, naturalness is of paramount importance.

3. *Holding the branches in place.*

Needlepoint ("sword-mountain") holders may be attached to the container with any of the new waterproof floral clays, or they may be left free so groups may be shifted later if a more pleasing position is found for the material it holds. The latter process is always followed by the Japanese and is excellent for practice work, for visual balance is usually identical with physical balance and the holder will obligingly (or disobligingly) tip over if a group is not properly balanced. Even small holders with heavy material will remain upright when the group is correctly balanced unless the container is moved or jolted.

There are several ways to handle a branch which is too heavy to grip the needles properly.

(a) Needlepoint holders are now on the market to which a branch can be attached by a screw in the bottom of the holder. (Diagram IV-B, #1.)

(b) The branch can be nailed to a small piece of plywood which can then be weighed down by a stone or by the holder used for the rest of the material. (Diagram IV-B, #2.)

(c) Gently hammer a Y-shaped stick and two heavy twigs firmly into a heavy needlepoint holder and then brace the branch against the crotch of the Y and lace wire across the top of the branch and around the tops of the Y and twigs to hold it firm. (Diagram IV-B, #3.)

4. *Shin.*

As in all types of Japanese arrangements, place Shin so its tip falls immediately over the point where the stem emerges from the water. Branches can be bent to assume sharper curves, as described in Chapter I.

Auxiliary branches in this central group should be added as heretofore, with Shin in the center. In all groups, the longest auxiliary branch will look best *behind* the main branch, with the shortest auxiliary branch in front of Shin.

For the sake of clarity, it should perhaps be repeated once more that each group is made up of three separate lines. However, fewer auxiliaries may be needed—or many more. Any number of auxiliary lines may be added to strengthen any of the groups, as long as each group retains the prescribed shape and no lines in the finished composition appear to be of identical height.

5. *Soe.*

If Soe is to be a more or less vertical line it may be placed either behind the Shin

[58]

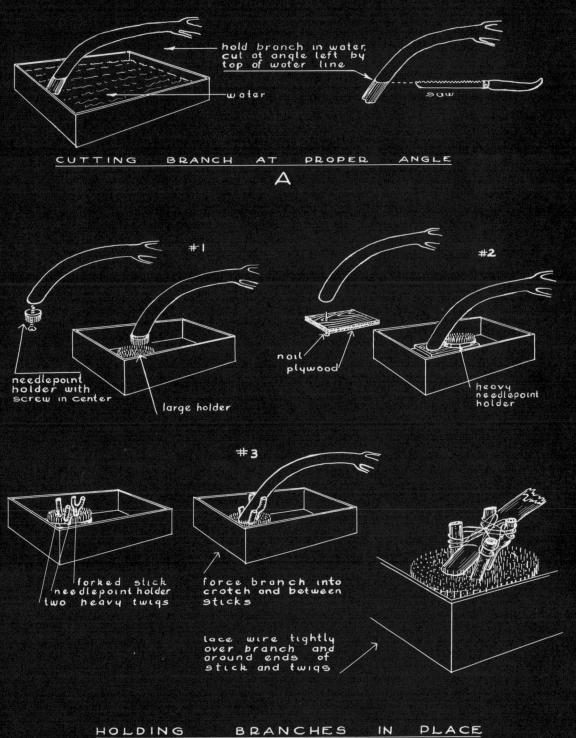

hold branch in water,
cut at angle left by
top of water line

water

saw

CUTTING BRANCH AT PROPER ANGLE

A

#1

needlepoint
holder with
screw in center

large holder

#2

nail
plywood

heavy
needlepoint
holder

#3

forked stick
needlepoint holder
two heavy twigs

force branch into
crotch and between
sticks

lace wire tightly
over branch and
around ends of
stick and twigs

HOLDING BRANCHES IN PLACE

B

DIAGRAM IV

group, as in Ikenobo designs, or to one side of it, as in Nageire. It should lean away from Shin at a thirty- to forty-five-degree angle, leaning toward the side and back, as in Ikenobo designs, or toward the side and front, or else its line should flow across the container as in a Nageire design.

If Soe leans out across the water in a water-viewing design it should follow the Shin line for a few inches before curving sharply away from it. Soe veers away from Shin fairly near the water for a water-viewing design and remains practically parallel to the water. In a cliff-viewing design, Soe follows Shin for about half its length before curving sharply downward toward the water—almost touching the rim of the container on the opposite side of the design.

Auxiliary lines may either be shortened to strengthen the base of the design or may follow Soe. However, the tips of all lines should follow the classic rule of pointing toward Shin, and the group should be roughly fan-shaped or triangular in form. Nothing should droop below the Soe line.

6. *Tai.*

Tai and its auxiliaries should be cut to a height which complements both Shin and Soe, binding the design together as outlined in construction details for either Ikenobo or Nageire.

In this school, unlike that of Ikenobo or Nageire, it is the placement of the main Shin group in the container, not the direction taken by Tai, that determines whether a Kansuike or water-viewing composition is male or female (a left-hand or a right-hand arrangement). If weight is concentrated on the right side of the container it is considered a male, right-hand, or master arrangement; weight on the left makes it a female, left-hand, or guest design.

Auxiliary lines for Tai vary considerably. The first auxiliary line is often the same length as Tai, since Tai reaches toward the front of the arrangement and is greatly foreshortened. As in other schools, the second auxiliary is always the shortest rib.

Tai should be a half-open bud, while auxiliaries may be fully opened flowers or well-leafed branches.

7. *Double arrangement.*

If the composition is to be made up of two widely separated groups with a "fish path" between them, Shin of the smaller group may be three-fifths to five-sixths the height of Shin in the larger group, or it may be shortened to any height that is in keeping with the material and fits the over-all proportions necessary to unify the design and bind the various parts together.

In a double-rooted design it will usually prove more satisfactory to have Tai of the larger group point forward, and Tai of the smaller group point toward the larger group.

Although the larger group should be scant enough not to crowd the smaller (Tai of this group should not come beyond center of container), the smaller group is nevertheless complementary to the larger one, and should therefore remain subordinate to it in every respect.

8. *Tome.*

A "stopper," "false-horizon," or "look-through" group may be added in either a double-or single-rooted design to thicken or deepen the composition. Tome should be placed behind Shin of the larger group and it should be sparse, since it "grows" on the north. This group should "look through" between Shin and Tai and its height may be half that of Shin, or it may correspond to the variation between Shin and Soe.

9. *Do.*

A fifth, very short, rather full "body" or "valley" may also be added if needed. Do should be placed in front of Tai and as close to Shin as feasible. It is the lowest group—the "valley"—and should consist of material that would normally grow nearer the ground than other material used in the design.

10. *Nemoto.*

In a double design there should be two clearly defined "roots" from which all material seems to be growing. In a single design, even though the groups may occupy more than one needlepoint holder, each *kind* of material should apparently be growing from its own root. All stems should be closely related at the base (while spreading naturally above) as if they were actually supported by a common root.

Tree material should show a well-defined nemoto, while bush material may have small branches added at the base to indicate its natural growing habit.

11. *Simplest order for inserting stems in holder.*

(a) If the longest line is Shin, establish Shin first; follow with Soe and Tai, then with the first and second auxiliaries of each group. While leaving enough room between the three main lines for necessary auxiliaries, be sure not to make the base of the design so loose that the composition appears to be falling apart.

(b) If the longest line is Soe, establish this first; follow with Shin and Tai, then with the first and second auxiliaries of each group. Leave sufficient room between the three main lines for auxiliaries, but keep the base of the design compact—to look like a naturally growing plant, or closely related plants.

(c) If a boku (heavy branch) is used, it is usually best to establish its position and angle first, then to proceed with the other material as outlined above.

(d) If a double design is to be made, establish the three main lines of the larger group, follow with the three main lines of the smaller group, then fill in with the auxiliaries for Shin, Soe, and Tai of the larger group and finally with the auxiliaries for Shin, Soe, and Tai of the smaller group.

In both single- and double-rooted designs Tome and Do (each with its own Shin, Soe, and Tai) are usually added last—if needed.

12. *Covering holders.*

Holders should be covered with material which would normally be found on the ground. Do not mass foliage unnaturally around the holders; instead, use interesting pieces of wood, moss, rocks, pebbles, or other suitable material.

If moss is not readily available, any evergreen that will not foul the water (such as lycopodium, or bunched needles of pine, cedar, cypress, juniper) may be tied in small groups with green thread and trimmed to look like moss. The material may then be arranged to drift out into the water in a natural manner. It should *not* form a stiff, compact mound.

[61]

To depict a quiet winter scene, nandina was arranged as a single "growing" group in the front section of a large container. The shape of the irregular base (beneath the blue-lined, off-white container) might also be interpreted as indicating the receding of water after seasonal rains.

Gnarled wood and mossy-looking rocks help balance the tall design and increase the feeling of age created by the clearly defined nemoto. Although "heavenly bamboo" is employed to convey congratulations, berried branches are *not* considered suitable for felicitous occasions and are usually accompanied by flowers of contrasting color for Tai. (If a tokonoma contains more than one flower arrangement, one of them customarily incorporates branches with berries.) (Photo: Fort Worth Photo Lab.)

A large cream-colored container lined in soft blue—the color of distant water—helps interpret another cliff-viewing arrangement in the Moribana style.

An old pine, clinging to a rocky ledge, leans out over the river far below, while a few roses find precarious footing among the rocks at its feet. The branch reaching forward and beyond the edge of the container helps to create the impression of a river flowing off into the distance. The placement of material toward the back of the container indicates a summer scene. (Photo: Lawrence Joseph.)

Three crimson-throated cyclamen with a few buds nestled in the foliage form a graceful "growing" group in an antique crescent-shaped bronze container held in place by a wise-looking, long-armed bronze monkey.

The texture of the interestingly shaped stick at the base of the Kakebana design harmonizes with the rough-textured wall, and repeats, in reverse, the swelling curve of the container. (Photo: John Hugelmeyer.)

Example of a Japanese Adaptation in a Contemporary Setting

A three-dimensional design incorporating basic working Ikenobo principles. However, more tulips have been used than are called for in a strictly classical design, which would emphasize the beauty of stems and foliage. Extra flowers were added because the fluid, exaggeratedly tall, precise curves typical of the Enshiu school would have been lost against this particular background.

The composition creates a pleasing flow of color, tying the soft rose shiki-silk walls of the contemporary bedroom into the deeper pink marble of the low window seat, with its delicate green cushion and jade ash tray. (Photo: Gottscho-Schleisner, Inc.)

"City by the River" is a composite picture specially designed to celebrate the National Council of State Garden Club's Permanent Home dedication in Shaw Gardens at St. Louis. The arrangement combines Nageire and Moribana principles as well as containers.

In an abstract, highly symbolic manner the dignity of the garden and the streamlined beauty of the tall buildings crowding against the river's edge are suggested by the placement of the two containers (one horizontal, the other vertical) and by the materials arranged as a single design. The past is symbolized by the gnarled, lichen-covered wisteria, the present and future by the delicate tendrils and budding blossoms. The low container with its broad expanse of water and lilies suggests both the river and the pools contained in the garden. Rising above the tall container, the diagonal pattern of the wisteria symbolizes a plane taking off in flight over the city.

The rhythmic circles suggested by leaves, budding blossoms, and velvety seedpods, as well as the heavy vine and fungus at the lip of the container (which strengthen the design), give an impression of perpetual life and movement. (Photo: *Photographic Arts.*)

Arranged in a shallow container, two groups of cattails, three yellow Dutch irises, and a few succulent leaves represent a quiet poolside scene under the shadowy leaves displayed through the frosted-glass panel. Japanese arrangers would feature one or two cattails with self-foliage rather than the two separate heavy clumps; however, additional strength was needed for the design to hold its own in this particular setting.

The cattails were carefully curved at the tips so the eye of the viewer keeps returning to the center of the over-all design (behind the glass) rather than having it follow the vertical supports.

The arrangement is slightly out of balance, the material having been moved from the left side of the container so the lines of the design would be clear in the photograph. Balance by placement is an all-important feature of Moribana designs, and Occidental adaptations allow great leeway in complementing elements present in the background.

The position of a design in the central portion of the container (from back to front, not from left to right) indicates either a spring or fall scene. In this arrangement, the inclusion of iris blossoms indicates a spring scene, with new growth rising vigorously from last year's spent cattails. (Photo: Gottscho-Schleisner, Inc.)

Five chartreuse "Fuji" chrysanthemums twine rhythmically around a windblown aspidistra "tree" in this very free interpretation of Japanese principles. Glass slag covers the cupped needlepoint holder (providing deep water in the shallow pottery container) and gives contrasting textural interest at the base of the design.

With slight re-adjustments the three levels of foliage could be made to conform to classic Japanese procedure; yet very definite rules govern the use of this material. Large leaves are usually used for the Shin and Soe lines and small leaves for Tai. Furthermore, the Japanese do not sanction the use of flowers with aspidistra. The combination is nevertheless effective for the Occidental home. (Photo: Lawrence Joseph.)

Hanging Designs

When a Japanese host hastily placed a morning-glory in a hollowed-out gourd, and hung the arrangement by the doorway to honor an unexpected guest, he unknowingly started a custom which has endured in his country ever since.

Prior to that time, and ever since the middle of the Edo Period, flower vases had occasionally been hung on the pillar of the tokonoma or in a tea-ceremony room to preserve the simplicity of the prescribed mood. Early records indicate that such designs were invented by the tea master Sen Rikyu in order to economize on space in tea rooms less than two meters square.

The ease of making a *Kakebana* arrangement—and the effectiveness of the design— was a boon to the busy host, for flower arrangement had gradually acquired an importance equal to the preparation of food. The popularity of "hanging flowers" kept pace with the growing use of flowers in the home, and special containers made their appearance in many new shapes. Decorative wall tablets were designed as backgrounds for hooked-up flower vessels, and played as important a part in some Kakebana designs as a base or stand did in other types of arrangements. (See photograph on page 89.) These wall tablets vary from those made of weathered wood or flattened polished bamboo to highly ornamental lacquered ones inscribed with short poems. Their original purpose was to protect the rare woods used in Japanese houses, and definite rules were devised governing their dimensions and placement. Most schools still frown upon their use on tokonoma walls, and plain black or the subdued tones of natural wood and bamboo are generally preferred.

In the more lenient schools, considerable leeway is allowed in the placement of Kakebana designs. However, they are usually found either on the back wall of the tokonoma or hung on one of its side pillars at eye level. Regardless of where the arrangement is hung the kubari, or forked holder, is placed so the single end points toward the guest of honor seated in front of the tokonoma. Thus, even when the design is hung on a side pillar, the guest is assured the most pleasing view of the arrangement. The lines of such hanging designs reach toward the scroll which usually occupies the middle of the back wall of the tokonoma (rather than toward the garden, as in other arrangements).

Many Kakebana containers are fashioned of the finest bronze and are cast in the shape of boats or designed to represent the varied phases of the moon. Porcelain containers are made with a flat side (to fit snugly against wall or post) and a hole for hanging. Other types, improvised from bamboo shoots, baskets, and gourds are used in many shapes and sizes. Regardless of whether a family in Japan enjoys great wealth or lives in humble circumstances, some sort of suitable container for a Kakebana arrangement is available.

As Kakebana became popular, simple designs designated the season, often the exact month, and sometimes, through further symbolism, a certain day of the month. Although the choice of containers was fairly flexible, bronze was favored in spring; porcelain was used to express the lightheartedness of summer; while a fine old basket, or weathered bamboo, was generally used in autumn and winter to help convey the impression of quietness and loneliness.

Boat-shaped containers, devised for the tea cult in the Momoyama Period, acquired new importance and many shades of meaning. The simpler suspended bamboo boats first used in the fifteenth century grew in popularity and were supplemented by bronze ones with fanciful shapes and distinguishing names. When hung lengthwise in the tokonoma with their prows toward the light (incoming) they welcomed a guest returning from a journey, celebrated a wedding, or announced some other auspicious occasion. An outward-bound boat (with prow away from the light) bade a friendly and sorrowful farewell to a member of the family or a friend about to depart on a journey. In these designs a line representing an oar swept gracefully from the stern of the boat indicating a wish for the voyager's safe and early return.

A full, sweeping curve of the Shin line in a boat design indicated wind in the "sails," the degree of the curve suggesting the comparative speed of the vessel. A safely moored boat, with sails furled, was indicated by a vertical Shin line. This also signified a contemplative mood—a mind as untroubled as the quiet waters. Such a boat usually held irises or reeds (which grow best in still water) and was customarily displayed on a flat board rather than in a hanging position.

Slender and delicate lines of plant material arranged in a boat hung high (well above eye-level) indicated a vessel some distance away on the high seas; more massive lines suggested a boat nearer home. (Diagram V-A.) If water was visible in the container this would suggest a leaking boat, so either the boats were hung above eye-level or the water was concealed in some manner—otherwise the arrangement might be construed as a wish to break off a friendship or as a bad omen for the coming journey.

Moon-shaped containers carried subtle messages of love as well as indicating the season of the year; often they would actually suggest the time of day when a family event would take place. A few leaves and an iris bud in a flat container hung high suggested a distant pond, while a design containing more foliage might be hung at

[77]

Many Kakebana customs developed as the art of flower arranging gained popularity in Japanese homes. Flowers given as presents were honored by display in hanging receptacles, so that they might gain further distinction by being looked up to. Sometimes a valued container was displayed empty, while flowers and shears were placed reverently beside it, and a simple Kakebana nearby paid further tribute to its age and beauty. Here the implication was that it would be presumptuous to attempt a design worthy of the superior qualities of such a receptacle. To the initiate, even deeper philosophic truths were conveyed by such a display: a rare and beautiful vase was in itself a symbol of perpetual harmony.

Here a long-lasting arrangement of ivy is featured in the container illustrated on page 67. Again a boku, or stick, ties the design in with the texture of the wall. This time the stick serves as a nemoto (root or trunk), adding weight to the center point of the composition.

The stick could also be used to conceal a small pot of earth so that trailing vines of ivy could actually be growing in an arrangement of this kind. Or, if sufficient light existed in the room, ivy could be rooted and grown in the water of the container. The vine, trained into attractive, curving lines, could thus provide a living background for seasonal flowers with short stems. (Photo: John Hugelmeyer.)

[78]

A bamboo "ship" with iris "rigging." The mellowed container (with lacquer lining) rests on two irregularly placed black lacquered boards, suggestive of smooth, untroubled waters.

Although the three flowers are in almost identical stages of development, other general Ikenobo rules as to shape and proportions have been followed in their arrangement.

A cleat in the deep window allows the ship to be hung when the outdoor scene and available material suggest such treatment.

Some kinds of iris bloom the year round in Japan and certain types are considered feminine, while others (because they are straight and graceful) are regarded as masculine. Every species possesses special characteristics, and the height established for the various leaves, blooms, and buds at each season of the year is the result of painstaking study of that particular plant's habit of growth.

Iris tectorum, or "roof" iris, acquired its botanical name because it is cultivated on thatched roofs in Japan to keep away evil spirits and to prevent the spread of disease (and only incidentally because its spreading roots help bind the straw together). Iris is also popular for congratulatory occasions and indicates patriotism because of its swordlike leaf. Leaves of the *Shobu*, or sweet flag, are placed in the bath during the Boy's Festival to instill the boy-bather with a warrior-like spirit. (The name Shobu even has a sound similar to that of the Chinese word meaning "contest" or "struggle to win.") (Photo: Gottscho-Schleisner, Inc.)

eye-level to suggest a pond nearer home. Every variation of every line, as well as the material used to achieve the design, had its own finely shaded meaning.

A long trailing vine with a knot in it (either natural or contrived) indicated the desire to keep a loved one by one's side, voiced the wish for the safe return of an honored guest, set the seal on a budding friendship, or expressed family loyalty or filial devotion —whichever the case might be.

Although purple wisteria was particularly beautiful in Kakebana designs, it was not used for important occasions, because of its quickly fading color and because of yet other, more subtle considerations. Since the tendrils twist both to the left and to the right (masculine and feminine, positive and negative), they express the necessary duality of existence, but the flower is considered unsuited to felicitious occasions because purple is the color of mourning. And as for white wisteria, the tendrils twist counter-clockwise; this does not suggest a harmonious relationship with the universe.

Yet in spite (or perhaps because) of the many traditional taboos connected with the use of wisteria, under certain circumstances the flower can be used to symbolize the gentleness and obedience which is characteristic of ideal womanhood in Japan. Correctly used, wisteria often tells a tender and moving story to the Japanese.

Willow, being a water-loving tree, is ordinarily featured in poolside designs; however, it may also be adapted to Kakebana. These "cliff-viewing" designs are sometimes used merely to emphasize the grace of the pendant or dangling (not weeping!) growth, but they usually tell a story as well. A willow branch may simply be used to nod over a quiet stream, but if it droops on both sides of it, mourning or bereavement is indicated. On the other hand a willow branch that trails down on only one side of the stream represents the wish for a long life, safe journey, or happy marriage.

Willow and red camellia are considered a suitable tribute to a beautiful maiden (the grace of her carriage is embodied in the willow, the beauty of her vivid coloring in the bright red and green of the camellia). However, care must be taken to incorporate more camellia buds than blooms in the design, for the flower does not fall petal by petal but drops bodily from the stem: fully blown blossoms will already suggest a beautiful life brought suddenly to an end.

The association of willow with the tree-frog dates back to the tenth century and is much like our own story of Bruce and the spider. Ono-no-Do-fu had spent many years trying without marked success to master the difficult art of calligraphy. On his sixtieth birthday he paused during a stroll through his garden to watch a tiny frog. The little creature made sixteen unsuccessful leaps before it finally reached its goal on a hanging willow branch. The nobleman, shamed by the courageous determination of the lowly frog, returned to his studies with renewed vigor and became one of the greatest calligraphers of his time.

Even today a pendant willow branch with a frog beneath is a favored decorative motif for a lacquered writing desk, or for a room used as a study, while Japanese floral compositions featuring willow often include a small bronze frog in an inconspicuous corner of the container. Sometimes the moral is suggested less subtly by featuring a willow branch in a Kakebana design and placing the frog on a small stand beneath it.

slow-moving
incoming boat
(PROW toward light)

fast - moving
outgoing boat
(prow away from light)

far-away boat
slender lines hung
well above eye level

boat at anchor
tall slender lines
(on flat board)

A

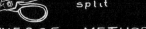
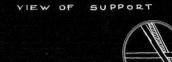

container

cut heavy twig
slightly shorter
than diameter
of container

split

hole for hook

SHIN

split end - OR - attach to twig
(of SHIN)   (with thread or
                    string)

flat side of twig

WEDGE METHOD OF HOLDING SHIN ERECT

B

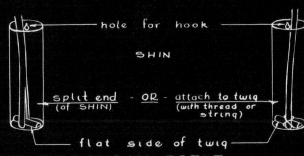

cut twig
slightly longer
than diameter
of container
wedge firmly
against sides

split end
OR
attach to twig
with string
thread or wire

tie for added
support

TOP VIEW OF SUPPORT

the nearer stem is attached to
LEFT end of supporting twig, the
farther LEFT it will emerge from
container

the nearer stem is attached
to RIGHT end of supporting
twig the farther RIGHT it will
emerge from container.

WEDGE METHOD OF HOLDING SOE (or TAI) AT DESIRED ANGLE

C

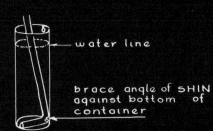
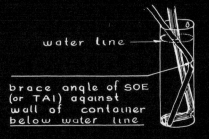

water line

brace angle of SHIN
against bottom of
container

water line

brace angle of SOE
(or TAI) against
wall of container
below water line

CRACKED—STEM METHOD OF HOLDING MATERIAL IN PLACE

D

DIAGRAM V

1. *Selecting the three main lines.*

The three main lines may be cut to either Ikenobo or Nageire proportions, whichever best conforms to the container, the material, and the position in the room where the design is to be placed.

Shin is usually somewhat foreshortened in Kakebana designs and is seldom more than the length plus the width of the container. If the container is suspended by a cord or chain which forms a triangle, the tip of Shin should conform to the apex of this triangle. (Diagram V-A.) If the container is moon-shaped, Shin is usually kept within the real or imaginary circumference of the circle. (See photographs on pages 77 and 81.)

Pendant material with a trailing Soe (or Tai) is most effective in Kakebana designs. However, it is well to remember that a line which trails more than two-thirds the distance between the container's rim and the floor will prove very difficult to balance, and (unless the arrangement is placed in a tokonoma) such a long line is apt to be in the way as well.

Tai should, as heretofore, be selected to harmonize with the length and shape of the other two lines.

2. *Cutting the three main lines.*

(a) If Shin is the longest line, follow directions given for Ikenobo.

(b) If Soe (or Tai) is the longest line, establish its length and angle first. Next cut Shin in proportion to the container (it must also complement the angle formed by the cord or handle). Then cut Tai (or Soe, as the case may be) one-third or two-thirds the height of Shin—whichever length the design seems to dictate.

Longest lines should be cut first; when adding strengthening lines, it should be remembered that a hanging design does not allow for as much weight as an arrangement in a standing container. No matter how graceful the lines (or how well they conform to the growing habit of material) the beauty of design will be lost if it appears too heavy for its support.

3. *Holding the branches in place.*

Material for shallow hanging containers, such as moons and boats, may be controlled with the aid of a properly fitted needlepoint holder and/or kubari as described in Chapter I.

In deeper containers the needlepoint holder may be set near the top, as demonstrated in diagram III. A kubari can also be used. However, narrow containers often require no formal holder of any kind. Material can be controlled by Japanese methods commonly used in authentic Nageire designs.

Shin is established first by the simple expedient of wedging a short split section of a heavy twig crosswise into the end of its stem. (Diagram V-B.) The twig is cut slightly shorter than the diameter of the bottom of the container and inserted in the split Shin stem with the flat side down. The flat twig, resting squarely on the bottom of the container, holds the stem erect, and the split allows the stem to take up more water.

[84]

If Shin has a fairly firm stem it will remain upright without reinforcing. Small or fleshy stems, however, will need help and can easily be secured to the heavy twig with thread or string, as in diagram V-B. They may be further braced, if necessary, as shown in diagram V-C.

With Soe and Tai the same procedure can be followed except that the twig or section of stem which will act as a support need not be split, and it should be cut *slightly longer* than the inside diameter of the container. The extra length is needed here because the twig will be wedged against the wall of the container instead of resting on the bottom. (Diagram V-C.)

If the stem is attached toward the left side of the supporting twig, Soe (or Tai) will reach out over the rim of the container at the left; if it is attached toward the right of it, then the line will emerge from the container toward the right of the design. (Diagram V-C.)

As it is seldom desirable to have either of these lines rise from the exact center of the container, neither Tai nor Soe should be attached to the center of the supporting twig.

In certain containers (particularly square ones) and with some woody material it may prove simpler to crack the branch or stem to form sharp angles, as shown in diagram V-D.

Success with this method depends upon careful measuring *before* the stem is cracked. For best results, the broken portion of Shin should rest squarely on the bottom of the container with both the cracked and cut ends braced against the side walls. The crack in Soe and/or Tai should fall below the water line (to ensure proper absorption of moisture) and the cut end should rest on the bottom of the container. (Diagram V-D.)

In narrow Kakebana containers, it is actually easier to control the material by either of the previous methods than with any of the usual mechanical aids, and practice along these lines is an excellent way to acquire proficiency in true Japanese techniques. A few experiments will usually convince the student of the desirability—and ease—of such methods.

4. *Shin.*

As in other types of Japanese arrangements, Shin should have a tip suggesting growth, and the branch should be arranged so the tip falls immediately over the point where the stem emerges from the water. The branch can be bent as described in Chapter I.

Auxiliary branches, if needed, should be kept close to the central line and conform to Ikenobo proportions. They should strengthen the main line rather than thicken the design.

5. *Soe and Tai.*

Directions given under Ikenobo or Nageire apply equally to Soe and Tai in Kakebana arrangements.

Auxiliary branches may not be needed in either group, since the effect should be of three swelling lines rather than three groups of lines. If used, however, auxiliary lines

[85]

A single spray of pine and a few pink azaleas cascade from a small bamboo container. Hung by a sunny window in a narrow room, this cliff-viewing Kakebana adaptation casts interesting shadows across the ancient wall tablet and the rough-textured wall. The tablet is woven of dried honeysuckle vines.

The small arrangement is given considerable importance by being placed so that the shadow forms an integral part of the design, both in the daytime and at night.

A good bamboo container will always show an odd number of growth rings or joints. A three-sectional container represents growth at different altitudes: the top section is used for mountain growth, the center for flowers of the hills, and lowest division for material found at sea level.

A two-sectional container with a shallow top (such as the one in the photograph) is said to signify the "dimly caught reflection of a blenched moon swung athwart a mountain lake!" (Photo: John Hugelmeyer.)

Cyclamen leaves and three short-stemmed yellow tulips are grouped with two pieces of sponge in a hanging gourd. The novel, free-flowing Kakebana adaptation was made for an informal basement room. The old raffia-trimmed gourd repeats the form of the floats on the fishnet in the doorway and acts as a foil for the rough textures of the sponges and the net. In color the container closely resembles the rope, but it also repeats the smooth texture of the tulip.

Sponges are easily washed, and as easily shaped. They can be used to form a permanent background for whatever suitable seasonal material the garden or roadside provides.

The gourd is the emblem of Li T'ieh-Kuai (one of the Eight Immortals), said to have spent his time in the seventh century wandering about the country on a magic horse which lived in a gourd on his staff. When needed, the steed emerged and Li T'ieh-Kuai increased it to the necessary size by spraying it with water from his mouth. The subject is a popular one with painters, who generally show a horse (or horses) in the process of being conjured from a gourd.

The gourd represents mystery, necromancy, longevity, science, and medicine, and was used as a charm to ward off "vile influence." (Photo: John Hugelmeyer.)

should not fill out the design; they should be used merely to strengthen either Soe or Tai.

Following the general rule, Kakebana designs are considered male (or right-hand) if Tai points to the right, and female (or left-hand) if Tai points to the left.

6. *Nemoto.*

In boat- or moon-shaped containers a well-defined nemoto will usually prove more satisfactory, while baskets and wall brackets often lend themselves to a freer treatment.

7. *Simplest order for inserting stems.*

Use a kubari and/or needlepoint holder, and if Shin is the longest line follow directions given for Ikenobo designs. If Soe or Tai is the longest line, then follow the procedure outlined for Nageire designs.

When using a split twig to support the Shin line, establish Shin first. Follow next with Soe. Turn the twig sideways to insert the brace in the container; then pull it up firmly against the sides of the container until Soe assumes the proper angle. (Diagram V-C.) Follow the same procedure with Tai.

As a rule, further support should not prove necessary; however, if extra bracing *is* needed, the Shin stem may be tied to Soe, and Tai wedged against both Shin and Soe as well as against the opposite wall of the container. (Diagram V-C.)

If you are using the cracked-stem method of support, instead of a twig, establish the Shin line first and follow with Soe, then Tai. Measure all lines carefully to be sure you crack the stems in the correct place to make the branches take the angle you want. (Diagram V-D.) Although some moisture will be drawn through the narrow portion of the stem (at points where the breaks occur), the material will last longer if breaks are kept below the water line.

After Shin, Soe, and Tai have been arranged, add any necessary auxiliaries. Unless the container is unusually large or the material is particularly unmanageable, it should not be necessary to crack stems or add extra braces to anything except the first two (or possibly three) lines in the design.

Although Japanese flower arrangers would frown upon the use of floral clay or Scotch Tape, one or other of these can be used (in a very small quantity) on the tip of the container to hold an obstinate branch in place. In informal leaning designs it is an easy matter to conceal such aids with a leaf or flower.

8. *Hanging containers.*

Kakebana arrangements are usually hung so that the center of the design (or nemoto) is at eye-level. As a rule this means that the holder, regardless of type, will not show. If necessary, however, it may be covered by methods already prescribed.

9. *Final check.*

(a) The design must be suited to the location. And check to see that it is placed so branches don't catch at people's clothes or hair as they pass.

(b) The tip of Shin should be in the classic position—over the point where the stem emerges from the water. All tips, leaves, and flowers should look up toward the central line in a natural "growing" group.

(c) Remove any drooping foliage, also flowers or leaves that overpower the three main lines. The design should appear airy and uncluttered.

[90]

V: MORIMONO

Designs with Fruits and Vegetables

A *Morimono* design—an arrangement of fruit and vegetables—is easily created at the last minute to honor an unexpected guest. Such compositions are considered an integral part of the art of flower arrangement in Japan.

The apparently casual placement of material on a tray (or on a plaque or table mat) suggests that the host hurriedly selected the best his garden had to offer and assembled it for his guest to enjoy. In view of this implication, the use of only seasonal fruit and vegetables, or of those slightly in advance of the season, is considered in good taste. They must be scrupulously clean and invitingly fresh in order to stimulate the palate as well as please the eye.

Although the Japanese manner of arranging fruit and vegetables is closely related to the early twentieth-century Moribana style of design, the use of this material for decorative purposes in the Orient dates back much further. Records show that table arrangements of fruit and vegetables existed in the Ming period in China (1368-1644), and it is likely that even earlier examples could be found.

The name Morimono—"profuse or heaped-up things"—is as misleading as its sister term Moribana—"profuse or heaped-up flowers." Like the water area in a Moribana design, about two-thirds of the tray or mat in a Morimono arrangement is left free of material.

These compositions are favored by many tea masters and are just as carefully thought out as the most formal arrangements. The tridimensional triangular Ikenobo principles are applied, and with a few minor exceptions the same rules are followed. Although the height of the tallest placement is seldom more than the width of the tray, the height and bulk of the rest of the material are kept in pleasing proportion to this Shin group in accordance with classic Japanese procedure.

As in other types of designs, two of a single kind of material can always be used (two representing the beginning of life), but with this exception odd numbers of fruits

[91]

Morimono designs can be extremely practical in winter months when flowers are scarce. Here five bronze saxifrage leaves from the winter garden, two black and orange hubbard squash (one in the rear of the design concealing a small bottle of water which holds the saxifrage stems), one russet and one golden yellow apple, and three yellow-green bananas add warmth and cheer to a dining room on a dark winter's day.

The mustard-colored pottery trencher is placed on a bamboo mat which matches the picture frame and harmonizes with the brass candlestick, the candle, and the tawny tones of the rooster. There is also an affinity of color between the arrangement and the Audubon print.

Firm apples and bananas on the green side were selected for the arrangement, and it lasted for several weeks without replacements. (Photo: John Hugelmeyer.)

or vegetables are called for. This rule affects not only each kind of plant appearing in the composition, but also the number of different varieties used in the design! (Four of anything is avoided, not only because it is an even number but because it signifies death.) The rule governing the use of uneven numbers seems arbitrary to Occidentals, but it will almost invariably lead to a better design.

Only culturally compatible material appears together in a Morimono arrangement, and self-foliage, or foliage closely resembling that of the fruits and vegetables displayed, is preferred. Every possible device is employed to emphasize the idea behind this kind of arrangement—that it was made on the spur of the moment, of materials found in the garden, for the enjoyment of a guest.

Sometimes a small branch bearing leaves or fruit is placed on the tray to give the composition a long line. The end of the branch is broken, not cut, to indicate the haste with which the material has been gathered. Such a branch, of "simple and quiet taste," may even be "arranged by the light of nature" or "placed attractively" on the tray or plaque without further embellishment.

Since Morimono material is used directly on a tray, plaque, or mat, textural relationship and color harmony between the fruits or vegetables and the container becomes doubly important. The designs have somewhat the feeling of a still-life painting, and, although considerable leeway is allowed, neither mechanical aids nor water are used by the Japanese. Any obvious attempt to prolong the life of the material would detract from the honor paid the guest.

Fruits are usually shown with other fruits, and vegetables with other vegetables. When more than one fruit of the same kind appears in the composition, the different aspects are brought out by featuring both the blossom and stem ends (Ying and Yang, male and female, the essential duality of life). The carefully washed roots and sprouting tops of vegetables similarly dramatize this variation which, in other designs, is subtly suggested by the sunny and shady sides of the foliage.

The surface texture, as well as the shape and color of all the parts, is carefully considered in selecting material. As with other plants, the outstanding characteristics of individual fruits or vegetables are carefully studied and emphasized in the design. Some fruits are striking because of their shape, others because of texture, color, or distinctive foilage. This applies also to vegetables; and the decorative merit may lie even in their roots.

In sanctioning Morimono arrangements, Ikenobo masters make a notable exception to their rule against the use of edible plants. Among vegetables whose parts "blend well to give a refreshing impression" one finds such gastronomic delicacies as lily bulbs and lotus rhizomes together with bamboo sprouts and yams. Favored fruits include not only melons, pomegranates, and pears, but also chestnut burs, lotus fruit, and certain kinds of palm.

Fruit and vegetable compositions have their own distinctive decorative value when used alone; however they are often displayed in conjuction with a *bonsai* (dwarfed tree), flower arrangement, scroll, or some other art object.

The natural beauty of Morimono designs is also favored in early spring when the composition is often enhanced by the addition of a few simple flowers or a blooming sprig from a fruit tree.

Quite a variety of apparently unrelated objects may be successfully combined if they possess the same underlying feeling. Contrasting textures and colors are essential, and surprisingly beautiful Morimono designs often feature an unusual stone, or a dramatic effect may be achieved with only a clump of grass, a dried lotus leaf or two, and a seedpod carefully grouped on an interestingly shaped tray.

Although Japanese arrangements usually include something green to suggest continued growth, spent growth is not looked upon as dead or depressing and seeds are highly valued. Locked in a shriveled, scentless husk slumbers the secret of life itself, representing not only the fulfillment of past cycles but also the promise of the future. Seeds symbolize the continuity of the universe, and thus appear again and again in designs created by this sensitive and highly imaginative people.

Construction Details for Making Designs with Fruits and Vegetables

1. *Selecting the material.*

After studying the fruits and vegetables that the garden or market has to offer, and bearing in mind the color scheme of the dining room or other area where design is to be used, the arranger must decide three things:

(a) Which fruit or vegetable is to be featured and what phase (stem or bloom end, root or leaves) is to be emphasized?

(b) What subordinate materials will best complement the main object? (It is simpler to use contrasting yet harmonious colors and textures, as well as a variety of shapes.)

(c) Will the material look best on a tray, mat, or plaque? (The color must also be considered in relation to the material and the setting.)

The material you choose should be in scale with the tray or plaque (or vice versa). And, for the sake of beauty as well as assuring longer life for the design, make sure the fruits or vegetables are as clean as possible and that they are not over-ripe.

A few suggested combinations of material for Morimono designs follow.

A twig bearing a grapefruit, narcissus bulbs (considered quite a delicacy), a few small chrysanthemums, and mushrooms—arranged on an oblong plaque.

Persimmons, mushrooms, and fern—arranged in a basket.

A cabbage, onions, grass (resembling onion tops), and beets with carefully washed roots and a few tender leaves still attached—arranged on a mat.

Bananas, grapes, and apples, with a branch of loquat foliage—arranged on a slender, leaf-shaped tray.

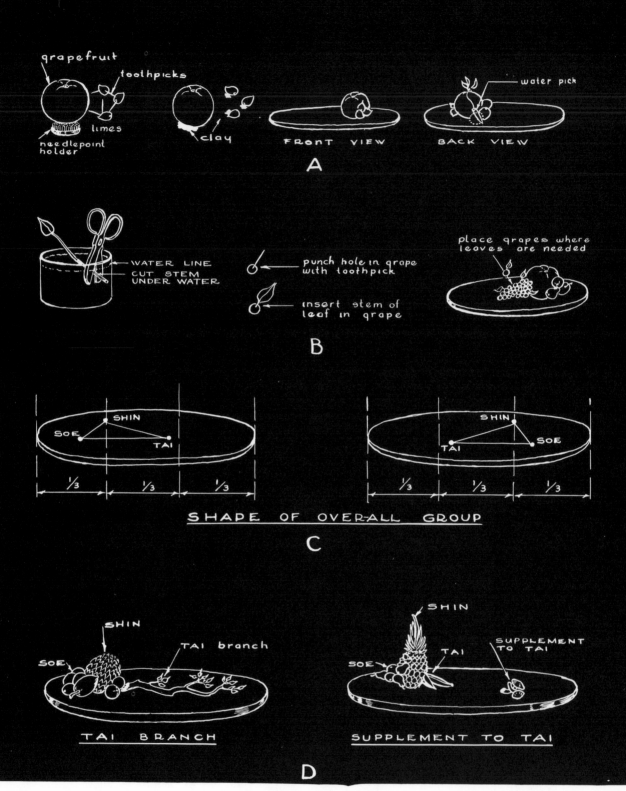

DIAGRAM VI

Lotus seedpod and root, two dried lotus leaves, and marsh grass—arranged on a bamboo raft or plaque.

Two turnips, a radish (both with fresh new leaves still attached), and a few small chrysanthemums—arranged on a burl.

Lily bulbs and small yellow chrysanthemums, with an almost leafless spray of bittersweet—arranged lengthwise across a polished board.

2. *Holding the material in place.*

Morimono masters patiently balance each piece of material against the others until the best position is maintained. However, there are short-cuts which make mechanics quite simple for the Occidental arranger.

A heavy needlepoint holder, floral clay, and a box of toothpicks will control even the most stubborn material. (Round cocktail picks are strong and easily concealed; furthermore, they are available in an assortment of colors.)

A holder may be either attached to a tray with clay, or left free so it can be shifted around to obtain the most pleasing effect. Once the main line, or heaviest object, is impaled on a needlepoint holder, or is firmly seated on the tray with clay, the lighter material may be added. This can be held in place with small pieces of clay, or with toothpicks. (Diagram VI-A.)

3. *Conditioning and preserving material.*

Authentic Morimono arrangements are made without water, and without any conditioning except cleaning. In the West, however, additional preparation and mechanical devices are used to prolong the life of the material.

Fruits and vegetables with roots or foliage attached can be soaked in water or crisped in a hydrator overnight to keep fresh-looking for a longer period of time.

Additional fruit or vegetable foliage is usually submerged in water overnight.

All signs of soil or spray should be carefully washed from flower stems and foliage before conditioning in the usual manner. (Warm water and a mild soap will remove even the most stubborn spray.)

Water for perishable material may be placed in a small cup holder, vial, medicine bottle, or water pick. Any of these miniature containers can be concealed in the design. (Diagram VI-A.)

Individual leaves or flowers are easily handled in the Japanese manner. After cutting the stems under water (to prevent air bubbles from forming and obstructing passage of moisture) insert stems into grapes, oranges, or any other juicy objects that form part of the composition. (Diagram VI-B.) (Grapes will often take on the aspect of raisins within a few days.)

4. *Shin.*

Usually some sort of fruit or vegetable with foliage attached, or a clump of grass or fern will provide the necessary height for the Shin line. As in all types of Japanese arrangements, the tip of this line should fall immediately over the heart of the design (in this case the heaviest part of the composition).

The length of Shin in Morimono designs is usually made equal to the width of the plaque, tray, or basket on which it is displayed. However, the *maximum* height of

Shin (as in other designs) is based on the growing habit of the plant, coupled with the visual weight of the container and material.

Even in Morimono designs, height lends drama—provided it does not overpower the rest of the design or throw it out of balance.

The heaviest part of the arrangement (concentrated at the base of Shin) should be placed well to the rear of the tray on an imaginary line dividing the tray into thirds. (Diagram VI-C.)

Shin with its auxiliaries should be roughly triangular, forming the back point of the over-all triangle, with sparsest support behind (reaching toward the side and back of the container) and with fuller, shorter auxiliaries in front. (Diagram VI-C.)

Any number of auxiliaries may be added to strengthen any of the groups, as long as each group retains the prescribed triangular form, and provided no material in the finished composition appears to be of identical shape and height.

5. *Soe.*

Soe usually occupies about two-thirds as much area as Shin and is slightly lower. It is customarily placed to either the right or the left and slightly in front of the Shin group.

The Soe group forms the front point of the over-all triangle and reaches toward the side and front of the container. (Diagram VI-C.)

6. *Tai.*

Tai and its auxiliaries, which should, so to speak, bind the design together, allow considerable leeway in their arrangement. Placed slightly in front of Shin, on the opposite side from Soe, the group is usually a little lower, slenderer, and *longer* than Soe (even though it is usually approximately one-third the actual *volume* of Soe).

Although Tai should retain a roughly triangular form, and only one-third of the tray is occupied by the base of the entire design, a branch with foliage or fruit attached may form a part of this group—reaching nearly to the far end of the tray. Or additional material may be placed at the opposite end of the tray as an extension or supplement to Tai. (Diagram VI-D.)

7. *Simplest order for placing material on tray.*

There is no definite rule here as to placement, but it will usually prove simpler to place the entire Shin group first, following with main objects forming Soe, then Tai.

Auxiliaries for these groups are then balanced against other material or attached to it (in the Occident) with clay or toothpicks. (Diagram VI-A.)

A flat spot may be cut on the bottom of a cabbage (or other heavy material) to help keep it in position. When juicy material such as pineapple is cut or impaled on a needlepoint holder, the tray immediately beneath it should be protected with foil or wax paper. However, if the cut is sealed with lukewarm paraffin no protection is necessary and the material will last longer.

8. *Final check.*

(a) Recheck the shape of the over-all design for clarity and make sure that no two identical forms in the composition run parallel to each other or show exactly

[98]

the same height or aspect. (Top, bottom, and side view should be featured where more than one of the same kind of fruit or vegetable is used in the design.)

(b) Add any auxiliaries that are necessary to make the over-all design pleasing from all sides. Keep in mind that a triangular form is best, and that each group should be in consistent proportion.

(c) The effect should be uncrowded. Material should occupy not more than one-third of the tray, and the main object, or group of objects, should stand out clearly.

(d) Remove any drooping foliage or any leaves that confuse the clarity of the triangular design. All foliage tips, and even roots, should look up toward the central placement (Shin) as if reaching toward the sun. (Roots treated in this manner not only avoid a sad, droopy appearance but also imply that all phases of nature recognize their part in the greater universe.)

Note: Construction details for Moribana designs will also prove helpful in planning Morimono compositions.

Branches of frost-touched mahonia foliage contrast airily with the heavy forms of the pineapple, artichoke, and pears in this gay Morimono design. A few Brazil nuts complete the grouping, which is set on a rosewood burl.

The mahonia repeats the coloring and graceful lines of the Hepplewhite mirror, and the sculptural quality of the artichoke and pineapple are well suited to the heavily carved table. The branches are inserted in small containers of water anchored with clay and hidden among the fruit. (Photo: John Hugelmeyer.)

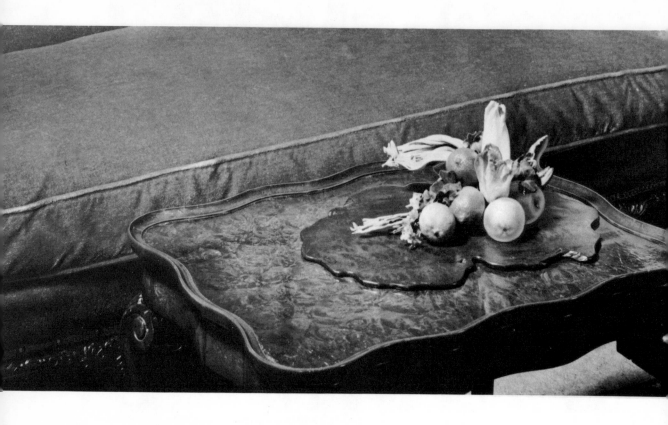

Two pale chartreuse clusters of endive, three limes, and two apples are grouped around a gnarled piece of wood. A small spray of ivy drifts down through the center of the arrangement, emphasizing the graceful lines of the soft gray wood and unifying the various other elements of the design.

The ivy (growing on its own roots) together with the driftwood forms a practical permanent background. Placed on a plaque, the arrangement can easily be moved when the table is needed for other purposes. (Photo: John Hugelmeyer.)

VI: **KAGO**

Basket Arrangements

In the fifteenth century a political refugee from troubled China made a *kago*, similar to the flower baskets in his country, and presented it to a Japanese military leader and tea master who had befriended him. The artisan requested that his humble gift be placed on a stand to enhance its value in the eyes of the leader. The powerful lord, pleased with the beauty of the gift and also by the humbleness of the artisan, ordered the basket to be placed directly on the matted floor of the tokonoma.

To this day baskets so displayed signify humility and most schools still prohibit their use with a *dai* (stand or plaque).

Fine examples of this art imported from China are passed down from generation to generation along with elegant bronzes and treasured family scrolls. A beautiful kago often compares in price with objects that seem of much greater value; even a basket of moderately fine weave usually brings several hundred yen.

The peony is considered particularly suited to basket arrangements, perhaps because it too originated in China. The long-lasting quality of the flower led to its being called the "flower of twenty days." Because of its large size, varied coloring, and difficulty of cultivation the peony was much prized by the upper classes. Its presence in the garden became a symbol of prosperity. In temples and palaces frescoes frequently show peonies accompanied by the peacock or Chinese lion, both of which creatures are emblematic of royalty or high birth and worldly possessions.

Another kind of basket originated in Japan. This is the *jakago*, or "stone basket." Anchored against most Japanese river banks, the jakago has become an integral part of the local landscape. The baskets, cylindrical in shape and crudely woven of bamboo, are filled with stones to protect the river's edge from swift currents. As might be expected, small replicas of the jakago—from ten inches to as large as three feet in length— were made for indoor use and became popular for displaying rushes or other water-loving plants. (See photograph on page 111.)

In Japan a basket of flowers is the emblem of Lan Ts'ai-ho (of the Eight Immortals), and the many connotations associated with it are somewhat confusing to the Occidental mind. A basket of flowers is the symbol of old age; it is carried by the patron saint of florists and it is also a symbol of delusive pleasures!

Chrysanthemums (which are used in this Nageire design) also have various special meanings. The flower was introduced from China and has been cultivated by the Japanese for more than fifteen hundred years. More than eight hundred varieties now exist in a total of about two hundred and fifty different colors. The sixteen-petaled form symbolizes the harmony of heaven and earth (seven is the number representing heaven and nine earth).

This variety is Japan's national flower and was adopted as the crest of the Imperial Family in the twelfth century. The petals radiating out from a common center symbolize the people held in unity by the Emperor, and when displayed in public places the bloom is covered with paper to keep it from profanation by public gaze! (Photo: *Photographic Arts.*)

Although many baskets were designed specially for hanging designs, others, fashioned for the floor of the tokonoma, are particularly suited to the informal character of wild grasses and to the lighter, airier kinds of flowers. The "seven flowers of autumn" (mentioned in collections of poems as early as the eighth century) are usually displayed in baskets. Following the traditional custom, seven of the many flowers blooming in this abundant season are selected to represent all the grasses and herbs of autumn. These simple designs which capture the essence of autumn are still placed in homes, shops, and offices throughout Japan, and bring the charm and color of the outdoor scene into sharp focus for laborer and gentleman alike.

Maple leaves have also become closely associated with autumn. When the goddess of the season tips her magic vial, splashing the world with vibrant color, the maple takes on new significance. It becomes a flower instead of a tree. Branches of maple leaves in a basket arrangement symbolize the waning years. The "In" or "shady" side, where green and yellow leaves predominate, is reserved for the guest of honor, while the host is seated on the "Yo" or "sunny" side, where red and brown leaves indicate a more advanced season. Wide baskets containing tall elaborate designs are favored for expressing the majesty of this transient beauty. The beholder returns in memory to the "burning splendor of a maple grove where playful breezes weave restless red and gold leaves into a brilliant carpet for the goddess to sit on."

A bare willow branch is also considered "compatible with a field of autumn in good pose," and is often used in a basket to express the nostalgic mood of the season. On the other hand, a budding branch of willow may be arranged to rise gracefully from a fine kago—and this, accompanied by a single early-blooming camellia, will symbolize the rhythm of spring's awakening.

Many very practical restrictions are applied to basket arrangements. As in other types of designs the plant material occupies only about a quarter of the container—never more than a third. Furthermore, the material must harmonize with the color, size, and shape of the container and it must be suited to carry out the basic idea or theme of the arrangement. Thus, for instance, evergreens and heavy, woody branches would not be suitably arranged in a basket that had originally been designed for the transporting of light-weight material.

Baskets are woven in shapes and textures that are suitable for the most formal kinds of plant material and designs; other baskets are made for coarser flowers and informal arrangements. Most of the better baskets contain a carefully fitted copper or lacquered receptacle for holding water. Frequently we find baskets which have purposely been designed to give a lopsided effect; the intention here is to suggest age or mellowness—the beauty peculiar to old things being highly praised in Japan. *Tabi* (which means "solitude" as well as the "rusting of things") indicates the last approving touch of nature, a stamp of approval granted only to those things which have withstood both time and weather. Mossy rocks, lichen-covered trees, and oxidized copper, as well as fine old baskets, all have tabi—the quietude and rich mellowness of antiquity.

When making an arrangement in a basket, the shape as well as the height of the handle must be carefully considered. The design can either stay well within the periphery of the handle or soar proportionately above it. In either case, the handle is part of the over-all design. Except when the entire arrangement is framed by the handle, many schools arbitrarily call for the Shin line to intersect the handle at a point representing one-third of its total length, while the Tai line is kept within the boundaries of the handle. Regardless of what part the handle plays in the design, at least two-thirds of it is usually left free. The arrangement should appear light and airy enough to be picked up and carried.

An exception to the above rule is the case of a basket arrangement of morning-glory. This vine is sometimes arranged with its delicate tendrils winding around the lower part of the handle. However, because of its short life span, the morning-glory is generally associated with mortality and is therefore used with reservation. Some schools sanction the use of morning-glory only in "hooked up" or "suspended" vessels and even go so far as to specify that with handleless receptacles the vine must cling to a bare bamboo cane or a twig of bush clover.

The white camellia often appears in kago arrangements. This is a short-lived flower too, but a few twigs picked in early spring will express austerity and simplicity, and a fleeting loveliness which the Japanese say provides the observer with as much food for thought as the "pure beauty of a literary sketch."

Banana leaves, although not considered suitable for felicitous occasions, are often grouped as though growing (with a wind-torn leaf for Soe) and placed in large handle-less baskets. Being a tree, the banana is not arranged in a basket which would suggest that it might be carried.

A simple basket arrangement expresses the pulsing spirit of the changing seasons; it has a just-brought-in-from-the-garden element that is always fresh and charming.

Construction Details for Making Basket Arrangements

1. *Selecting the material.*
Carefully consider the size, color, and textural relationship between container, material, and the place where the design is to be placed.

Several things must be borne in mind:

(a) Baskets were originally designed for carrying light-weight articles and therefore call for arrangements with less visual weight than do other types of containers of similar size and color.

(b) Handles were originally designed for carrying baskets, and a composition must take this into account. The handle is considered an integral part of the design and at least two-thirds of it should be left free of plant material.

(c) Baskets look particularly well with bold or clearly delineated plant material,

In this interpretation of a Japanese river-bank scene a pair of miniature stone-baskets (*jakago*) filled with pebbles were placed on a raft of weathered wood. A few cattails and a single early-blooming narcissus make up the larger group, while tiny leaves, sprouting from the far end of the jakago, create the illusion of distance.

For its illumination the arrangement was entirely dependent upon artificial light. Thus the natural shadow (which deepens and adds drama to the design) became an integral part of the composition. The smooth black pebbles spilling out of the baskets match the color and texture of the formica chest, while the cattails and the larger stone at left are in keeping with the cruder texture of the sand-colored wall.

Centuries ago Ikenobo masters worked out very careful patterns governing the use of narcissus. The flower was called the "child of two seasons" (pushing up through the snow, it indicated the fertility of life still hidden in the ground). Narcissus symbolizes maidenly beauty, simplicity, strength, courage, and purity; it is also used as an emblem of mirth and joy. The flower increases rapidly; it therefore indicates prosperity as well as fertility and is used at weddings and other auspicious occasions.

Early narcissus and fruit blossoms indicate wistfulness, a yearning for eternal youth. Narcissus with bamboo speaks of beauty in discord; with pine it speaks of simplicity and elegance. (Photo: John Hugelmeyer.)

A picnic basket suggested a pleasing Moribana adaptation. Roadside grasses and a gnarled stump were used, with black-eyed Susans flowering over the basket rim.

The "woodsy" design created a splash of warm color, and the basket brought memories of family outings to mind.

With slight adjustments the design could be turned into a "seven flowers of autumn" interpretation—a combination of late-blooming flowers typifying autumn which dates back several centuries and is still very popular in Japan. (Photo: *Photographic Arts.*)

Three lines of spiraling eucalyptus rise above the handle of a silver basket, while a similar group cascades down over its lip. Between these stems, and carrying out the main line of the design, are a dozen roses. To obtain various sizes of bloom, the roses were treated as described on pages 121-22.

The three levels of material, as well as the curves, conform quite closely to Ikenobo principles. The design was created for the end of a long buffet table in a large Victorian dining room. The mirrored base helps to balance the tall lines of the design, while the reflection in the mirror gave the composition additional interest and was in keeping with the damask cloth used for the buffet. (Photo: Fort Worth Photo Lab.)

as opposed to fussy flowers which often detract from the patterned texture of the basket and give the design a "busy" look.

(d) Baskets can be found which are suited to formal flowers as well as to cruder or wild types of plant material.

(e) A fine old basket may equal the elegance of an antique bronze usubata. However, care should be exercised in making selections because baskets, though woven of identical material, may vary materially in quality, according to workmanship and shape, or both.

2. *Holding material in place.*

Construct the composition in a way which best conforms to the shape of the container, bearing in mind the type of design (Ikenobo, Nageire, Moribana, Kakebana, Morimono) best suited to the location where the arrangement will be used.

3. *Final check.*

(a) Does the material suit the shape and texture of the basket?

(b) Check for visual weight, and remove any material that overpowers the container or interferes with the rhythm of the design. Could the basket be picked up by the handle (if it has one)?

(c) As in all Japanese designs, see that the three groups (Shin, Soe, and Tai) are clearly delineated and that no two lines appear identical in height.

VII: CHABANA

Arrangements Featuring a Single Flower

The embryo of the custom known to us under the misleading name of "tea ceremony" was originally imported from India, but is not now recognized by the land of its birth. As practiced in Japan, the tea ceremony is based on the teachings of Zen, which emphasize humility, the unity of man with nature, and the harmony that exists among all living things. The simple serving of a cup of tea in harmonious surroundings is entailed, with all the work pertaining thereto done by the host himself—either actually in the presence of the guests, or while they wait in an adjoining room. Every act, every gesture, has its own special meaning, as do the floral design and arrangement of everything used for the occasion.

Chabana arrangements should express a spirit of humility, and many designs feature a single seasonal bloom accompanied by its leaves. Sometimes the austere arrangements are composed of a spray from a flowering shrub, or (if in keeping with the season) a bud may be added to suggest continuing life and activity.

While such arrangements are not *limited* to one flower, simplicity is all-important for in simplicity there is beauty, and in beauty the divine, according to the teachings of Zen. The creative skill apparent in this type of design is highly regarded. The flower is placed in a "smart and elegant fashion," and should have a "feeling of frankness" without giving a "sense of worldliness."

An unpretentious container (preferably bamboo or a simple basket mellowed with age) sets the mood. The Shin line in an unassuming one-flower design is usually reduced to not more than one-half the height or width of the receptacle. Thus the single bloom does not express vigorous growth; instead it conveys the "inward peace and enlightenment of nature's twilight profundity." For evening gatherings, a white flower is prescribed.

The Japanese consider culture "a bouquet of beautiful flowers dedicated to mankind by nature." They do not look upon poverty as an excuse for breaches of good breeding and refinement (nor does wealth give leeway in either field). Nature and culture are inseparably united, and flowers symbolize the meaning behind life and the universe. A knowledge of tea and flowers are two of the cultural requisites which are used throughout life.

Devised by men of culture for the benefit of their fellow men, the artistic conceptions and philosophy associated with the tea cult provided a means of escape from the stress and strain of life. Its followers acquired poise, peace of mind, and strength of character. The tenets of flower schools and the tea ceremony were woven around ideals closely allied to our Ten Commandments, and as we strive to live up to Christian beliefs so do Zen followers try to follow the deeper meanings and shades of meaning implied in the rituals of the tea cult. Their philosophic precept of beauty teaches man "to see a world in a grain of sand and infinity in a flower."

Through nature—represented in a simple, symbolic plant form—life as well as earthly desires are forgotten and man returns to his natural state (resembling that of plants and flowers). When the mind is cultivated and evil is wiped from the heart, innocence is reborn. The pure state of soul and body is reawakened; the harmony lost in Eden is restored. Thus divorced from the turmoil of life, man stands aloof from all passion and hatred (like an iris flowering beside a woodland stream). Uprooting desires (which spread like weeds) enables wisdom to flourish, and the mind, freed of care, enters the Land of No Worry. Care and work are purified, man rises (like the lotus) triumphant from the dank bog of worldliness to pure beauty and supreme joy.

The "elegant amusements" (tea ceremony and flower arranging) stress love for the quietude of nature as opposed to strife. Through them even the Samurai—who value bravery above all else—momentarily forget war and lose themselves in the joys of peace.

The limited material in a Chabana design must interpret the occasion silently and with unchanging pose, conveying joy, sympathy, sorrow, loneliness—always with due regard to the season. The inanimate actors in the vase resemble those employed by the painter in his interpretations. However, art is regarded as an important auxiliary of ethics and religion—not an end in itself.

All Japanese floral designs have their roots in the old Ikenobo triangular, tridimensional principles. The same rules (based on centuries of intensive study) may be applied alike to a single rose and its leaves, or to multiple compositions incorporating twelve-foot branches.

The tea ritual infiltrated through the Imperial Court down to the people and, like its sister art the Noh drama, has undergone few changes since it was first perfected in the twelfth century. However, during the seventeenth and eighteenth centuries many different schools sprang up. While Chabana arrangements were featured, by these new schools, as a rule the designs closely resembled the Nageire style. However, a bit more restraint was called for than in the usual "naturalistic styles," yet considerably less rigidity than was expressed in the elaborate Ikenobo forms of arrangement.

In its truest sense Chabana is a simplification—a carefully worded understatement —of the old complex temple designs.

[116]

Construction Details for Making One-Flower Arrangements

1. *Selecting the material.*

As in preparing other types of arrangements, choose a container that is suited in size, shape, color, and texture to the flower being used. And consider the design in relation to the place it is to occupy in a room. Bear in mind that considerable importance may be gained through the addition of:

(a) a suitable base;

(b) a bud; or

(c) an interestingly shaped stick, stone, or bare branch.

2. *Cutting the stem.*

Study the flower and the foliage in detail before cutting the stem, and consider further two things:

(a) How long a stem and how much foliage is available.

(b) Whether the flower will look best arranged low in the container framed by foliage or near the top of the design. If in doubt, follow the rule of placing the flower so that its normal growing habit is interpreted as nearly as possible.

Cuts made on the stem of a rose, chrysanthemum, gardenia, or any flower with side foliage should be done on a slant, immediately above the point where the leaf joins the stem. This enables you to take full advantage of available foliage. (Diagram VII-A.)

Judicious cutting will often assure *one* placement which provides *two* of the required levels at the same time. In other words a flower will take one level, and a leaf (on the same stem) represents another. Superfluous leaves or length of stem are then cut off. (Diagram VII-A.) After a cut is made, the scar can be disguised by rubbing a little dampened dirt or cigarette ash over it with your finger.

3. *Shin.*

Even in this simple type of arrangement the most pleasing balance is achieved by placing Shin so its tip falls immediately over the point where the stem leaves the water.

Shin should be cut as long as the material will allow, though it must be remembered that a two-thirds differential in height should exist—following classic rules—between the Shin, Soe, and Tai lines.

As in other designs, Shin should give a vigorous feeling, Soe should complement Shin, and Tai should bind the design together.

4. *Soe.*

The Soe line should be about two-thirds the length of Shin, arranged slightly to the right (or left) and either a little in front or a little behind the main line, according to what seems best for the material and the place the design will occupy in the room.

5. *Tai.*

This is usually made about one-third the height of Shin and is placed on the opposite side of the design from Soe.

[117]

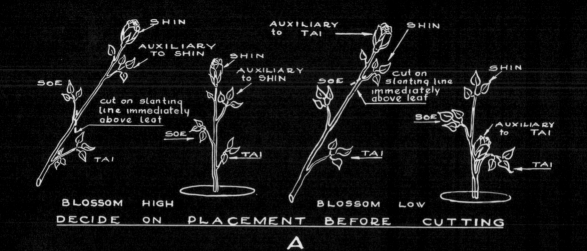

SHIN

AUXILIARY TO SHIN

SHIN

AUXILIARY TO SHIN

SoE

cut on slanting line immediately above leaf

SoE

TAI

TAI

AUXILIARY to TAI

SHIN

SoE

cut on slanting line immediately above leaf

SHIN

SoE

AUXILIARY to TAI

TAI

TAI

BLOSSOM HIGH

BLOSSOM LOW

DECIDE ON PLACEMENT BEFORE CUTTING

A

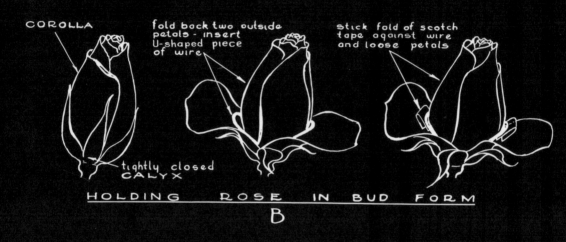

COROLLA

fold back two outside petals - insert U-shaped piece of wire

stick fold of scotch tape against wire and loose petals

tightly closed CALYX

HOLDING ROSE IN BUD FORM

B

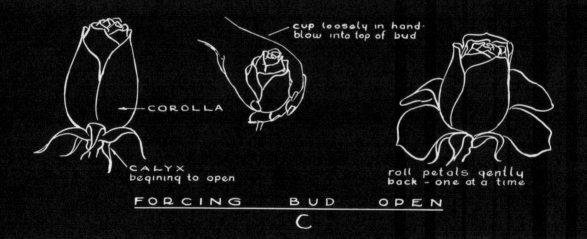

cup loosely in hand - blow into top of bud

COROLLA

CALYX begining to open

roll petals gently back - one at a time

FORCING BUD OPEN

C

DIAGRAM VII

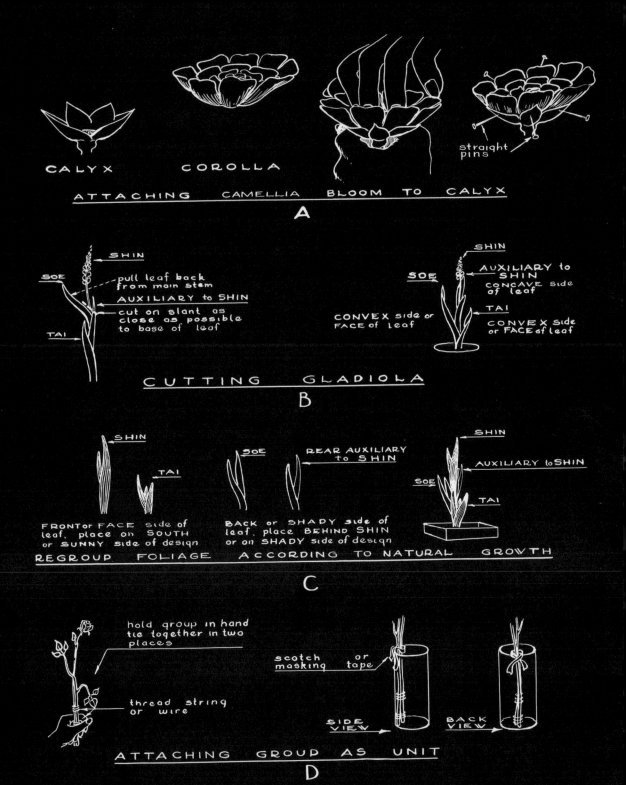

CALYX   COROLLA   straight pins

ATTACHING CAMELLIA BLOOM TO CALYX

A

SHIN
SOE
pull leaf back from main stem
AUXILIARY to SHIN
cut on slant as close as possible to base of leaf
TAI

SHIN
SOE
AUXILIARY to SHIN
CONCAVE side of leaf
TAI
CONVEX side or FACE of leaf
CONVEX side or FACE of leaf

CUTTING GLADIOLA

B

SHIN
TAI
SOE
REAR AUXILIARY to SHIN
SHIN
AUXILIARY to SHIN
SOE
TAI

FRONT or FACE side of leaf, place on SOUTH or SUNNY side of design

BACK or SHADY side of leaf, place BEHIND SHIN or on SHADY side of design

REGROUP FOLIAGE ACCORDING TO NATURAL GROWTH

C

hold group in hand tie together in two places

thread string or wire

scotch or masking tape

SIDE VIEW

BACK VIEW

ATTACHING GROUP AS UNIT

D

DIAGRAM VIII

6. *Placing and holding the material in the container.*

Any suitable mechanical aid and any order of insertion previously described may be followed when making a Chabana design. Or (except where strap foliage is being featured) the material may be carefully grouped in the hand and then placed on the pin holder as a complete unit.

In a tall container the unit may be attached to the lip of the vase with Scotch Tape or masking tape. (Diagram VIII-D.) Make sure, however, that the stems are well covered by water.

7. *Final check.*

The design should be triangular, following the standard rule of showing three distinct levels of material. It should give the feeling of a single growing plant.

(a) Check the three levels for clarity of line and see that the tip of Shin is vigorous and correctly placed in the design.

(b) Check the shape of each group. The tips should form a triangular pattern, and in turn each group of tips should form a triangle outlining the main shape of the design.

(c) Be sure none of the foliage is drooping unattractively. Leaves should face Shin, the tips and front (glossy or sunny side) of the foliage looking up toward the sun as if actually growing.

Note: Here again, the construction details already given for Ikenobo and Nageire arrangements will prove helpful.

Suggestions for Preparing Various Flowers

Rose

Many different designs may be made with a single rose. The illustrations on these pages show several possibilities. Even in Japan, the classic schools now make roses an exception to the taboo against plants with thorns, so even the purist can use roses in "authentic" Japanese designs.

Roses in bud are useful time and time again. If there is a choice of bud, select one that is firm to the touch—one where the calyx is still lying flat against the corolla, or petals. (Diagram VII-B.) The flower can be kept in bud indefinitely by either of the following two processes.

The first method calls for the slightly beaten white of an egg. Pull the outside petals back and cover them generously with the mixture where they overlap each other. Place the petals back in position and hold the bud firmly in your closed hand until the egg white sets sufficiently to hold the petals in place.

[120]

The alternative way is to cut two one-inch pieces of fine wire and bend these into a U or hairpin shape. Force the two outside petals of the bud back and insert the U-shaped piece of wire through the rest of the petals and down into the heart of the bud. (Diagram VII-B.) Conceal the wire by folding a small piece of Scotch Tape *with open ends down* (sticky side facing petal and wire loop). Press the ends of the tape against the wire loops and the loose petals, then hold the bud firmly in your closed hand until the tape adheres to both the outside petals and the main part of the bud.

Florist roses usually all have heads in bud form, and a good design calls for variety. A bud may be forced into bloom in the following way. If there is a choice, select a bud that is soft to the touch, and in which the calyx has started to curl back from the corolla. (Diagram VII-C.) If this is not possible, place the stem of the bud in hot water for an hour or two, first protecting the bloom from steam by wrapping it loosely in newspaper. When the water reaches room temperature it should be replaced with water that is not boiling, but hot enough so the hand would redden if held in it.

As soon as the bud appears soft, cup the bloom in your hand and blow hard into the top of the bud. This will loosen the outside petals, which can then be rolled back carefully over the thumb and forefinger. (Diagram VII-C.) If only the topmost petal is folded back each time and the petals are worked loose by continued blowing, each petal may be forced back firmly without tearing. The petals will remain in this open position.

These processes may sound drastic but they will have little effect on the life span of the rose *provided* hands are dampened in cold water before handling the bloom. The latter procedure, which prevents the oil and warmth of hands from damaging blossoms, should be followed before touching any kind of bloom. When hands are kept cool and moist, even camellias, gardenias, and magnolia blooms may be successfully handled.

Camellia

Designs using one camellia bloom and three and a half leaves are much favored by the Japanese. As mentioned earlier, four of anything (leaves or flowers or pieces of fruit) are not used, since four is the number of death.

For those not living in areas where camellias grow outdoors, the flower may be expensive. This makes the use of one flower extremely practical. The life of a camellia can be prolonged by sprinkling the bloom sparingly with table salt, covering it with damp paper towel, and placing it in a hydrator or in any airtight container in the refrigerator for an hour or two.

Even a blossom that has already fallen from the calyx may be enjoyed for several days if it is reattached with pins to the calyx and then treated in this manner. It is necessary only to insert three straight pins—or four if the blossom is particularly large or heavy—from the outside of the calyx, through the corolla to the other side of the calyx. (Diagram VIII-A.) Attaching the corolla to the calyx in this manner will also prevent the blossom from falling.

An arrangement showing how dramatic the placement of a single flower can be when surrounded by its own foliage. The outline of the leaves follows the prescribed Nageire triangle; this contrasts with the circular shape of the container and the rose.

The center of the container, countersunk (like the well in the saucer-like top of a usubata), is quite deep; thus the needlepoint holder lodged in it is concealed from all sides.

Even arrangements incorporating only one bloom must give a feeling of vitality and growth. No matter how simple the composition, it should be rhythmic and clearly defined. (Photo: Gretchen Harshbarger.)

The rose and foliage used in the preceding illustration were taken out of the container and placed in this narrow-neck vase. With the addition of the thick, curving twig at left and a flat stand set under the vase, an entirely new design was created. The long curving line starting at the top of the twig continues down around the vase and out along the front edge of the stand.

Roses are a comparatively new introduction to Japanese floral designs, but are now frequently used. Because they bloom in any season their frail, ephemeral beauty has been likened to a slender, witty, beautiful (but nervous!) woman.

Combined with pine, roses signify everlasting spring; with bamboo they represent virgin purity and peace. With plum this queen of flowers symbolizes the ideals of Japanese woman-hood. (Photo: Gretchen Harshbarger.)

A single fully opened rose is framed by its foliage and buds. The height of the tallest stem (the bud was originally part of the single cluster) is in suitable proportion to the height of the container. An irregularly shaped base balances the forward thrust of the rose and gives added importance to the whole design.

It makes a useful study on its own to compare the effects of arrangements made with and without the use of a base or stand. Many different stands are shown in the arrangements throughout the book, and the choice of yet other shapes should be explored in the shops that cater to a flower arranger's needs. The right stand will almost invariably give the finishing touch that a distinctive arrangement requires. (Photo: *Photographic Arts.*)

One rose (this time placed high in the design) is balanced by the weight of the pitcher and by the single carefully selected clipping of foliage which provides the other two customary levels for a Nageire arrangement. The placement of leaves emphasizes the flow of the pitcher's spout on one side and the slender lines of the handle on the opposite side.

The design was carefully built on Japanese triangular principles, yet a pleasing Hogarth curve is discernible. This starts at the tip of the lightest rose petal, follows down the outside of the left-hand leaves, moves across to the right-hand leaves, and continues down through the handle and diagonally across the container to the curving base.

A suggestion of this "beauty line" or "lazy S," may be found in almost any Oriental design, regardless of the medium, for the swelling curve of a Hogarth line represents only a slight stylization of many patterns created by nature herself. (Photo: Gretchen Harshbarger.)

A single flowering gladiolus, arranged in an antique bronze usubata of the Enshiu school with side bud and self-foliage is adapted to the prescribed Ikenobo principles. Black pebbles cover the needlepoint holder (in the flange of the saucer-like top) and the teakwood base gives added importance to the simple design.

The gladiolus (selected because of its side bud and vigorous foliage) had a straight and uninteresting stem. However, a piece of wire (#16) forced into the bloom stalk (after it was cut to the correct length) made it easy to bend the stem into the rhythmical line shown in the photograph. The leaves, carefully selected and cut for each placement, were grouped so that their convex sides hugged the three main directional lines (Shin, Soe, and Tai) and appeared to be growing from the same thick stem.

Additional foliage materially simplifies any one-flower design. And florists will often furnish extra foliage such as gladiolus leaves without charge, since they usually throw it away. (Photo: *Photographic Arts.*)

Gladiolus

When a single gladiolus is used in a Chabana arrangement, the cutting should be done very carefully so that all possible foliage is preserved. Leaves should be arranged naturally around the flower stalk, with the concave sides facing the Shin line as they would if the plant were still growing. (Diagram VIII-B.)

Iris, Narcissus, etc.

The most effective arrangements of iris, narcissus, and other material with similar growing habits are usually those which feature the striking straplike foliage rather than the bloom. Therefore, if sufficient foliage is available, these plants lend themselves admirably to one-flower designs.

Leaves for this type of material should be carefully taken apart and regrouped according to the nature of the plant. (As they grow only the "fullness" is represented, but to give completeness the three-tenths "emptiness" must also be apparent, as indicated in Diagram VIII-C.)

The usual procedure calls for the Shin and Tai groups to be placed with the fronts (sunny sides) of the leaves facing the arranger. Other groups, with their female (shady) sides facing the arranger are used for the Soe line and for the rear auxiliary to Shin. (Diagram VIII-C.) However, these placements will vary according to whether Soe is placed behind or in front of Shin, and also according to the number of leaves available and the natural growing habit of the particular plant being used.

It is especially important in this simple type of design that the arrangement look natural. And, since even the different species of iris vary tremendously in their leaf grouping and spacing, a few minutes spent studying the growing habit of the plant before taking the leaves apart will save a lot of "wondering what is wrong with the design" later on.

The single flower in a Chabana design is usually placed in the Shin group or as part of Tai (according to the season and the nature of the plant being arranged).

Early spring foliage is usually longer in comparison to the short-bloom stalk, and becomes proportionately longer as the season advances.

[132]

TOKONOMA

Designs Incorporating Other Art Forms

According to most authorities the recessed alcove in Japanese living rooms evolved through Zen teachings, which called for a wall hanging and a floral offering during the practice of meditation. However, some scholars trace the origin of these alcoves to the bed place of the *kami* or "superior," an area reserved for the kami to sit in, and a recess set aside for the image of someone noble or superior before whom flowers were respectfully offered.

The alcove, originally known as *oshi-ita*, is described by students of the Youshimasa Period (1435-1490) as a family altar. It is further described as a vertical area reaching from ceiling to floor, dedicated to the memory of Buddha, where "candles illuminated the sacred image hung on the back wall, incense burned quietly, and a bowl of flowers offered silent honor to all the family held dear."

The present name, *tokonoma*, evolved after *tatami* (mats made from compressed straw and rushes) came into general use as a covering for the alcove floor.

During the Heian Period, or Period of Peace (from the eighth to the twelfth centuries) all the arts flourished in Japan, and by the early part of the thirteenth century flowers were arranged in the home as well as in the temples. However, it was not until the fifteenth century that Senjun (twenty-sixth master of Ikenobo) adopted the simplicity of the Nageire (later known in the Ikenobo school as *Shokwa*) for use in the tokonoma. He drew up rules for Rikkwa and Ikenobo as well as Nageire and wrote treatises on all three styles of arrangement.

Through his teachings Senjun did much to bring about the changes that made the tokonoma (in its present form) a part of Japanese dwellings. In humbler homes it took the place of a separate room set aside for meditation.

The Japanese now use flower arrangements in stores, offices, halls, and other places where they are found in the West, but their true place is still in a temple or the tokonoma of the drawing room. Every dwelling, whether temple, palace, or poor man's hut, has this ornamental alcove or recess in the principal room. There are definite rules as to its dimensions. For instance a twelve-by-fifteen-foot room calls for a three-by-six-foot alcove regardless of how large or simple, how pretentious or humble the house may be.

A large home may have an adjacent recessed area with an ornamental shelf, or two arranged stepwise, and sometimes a miniature cupboard is contained in it as well. Such alcoves originally held a writing box, together with a bronze incense burner (symbol of ancestral worship), rolled scroll (symbol of calligraphy, painting, and truth), or some other related object. Today wealthy families may still devote an entire room to the tokonoma with its sets of nearby shelves; however, the adjoining study is now usually part of the living room and serves a decorative purpose.

Although the design of Japanese houses is still governed by the tokonoma, its role is primarily aesthetic. Built at right angles to the garden—which is always south of the house—the tokonoma occupies a corner of the room, has either a polished or a lacquered floor, and is designed with one angular and one round pillar of rare wood. Since the Japanese sit on the floor, it is necessary to raise the floor of the tokonoma only a few inches so the objects displayed in it may be seen to advantage.

In order to give a feeling of completeness, Japanese houses and gardens are customarily designed as single units. The ideograph for "home" is compounded of "house" and "garden"; the two flow into each other, merging into a single organic whole. Broad, open verandas cling to widely projecting rooms with sliding walls; soft, slate-colored roofs curve to repeat the forms of tree branches; upswung eaves reflect the shapes of growing things.

Both indoors and outdoors, natural colors play a very important part. Paint is used only on shrines (where railings and gates are lacquered). Natural wood and natural-colored fibers form most of the backgrounds, and wood is sometimes charred to develop a soft sepia patina which gives the impression of age, in keeping with the unity of man and nature. The Japanese garden is designed to be looked at while one is seated comfortably before the tokonoma; it is not created for exercise.

As in flower arrangements, both house and garden may be Shin (formal), Gyo (semi-formal), or So (informal). The architectural feeling of each portion of the house is repeated in the adjoining garden, interior decor, and style of flower arrangement, as well as in other branches of ornamental art.

Stately, decorous Shin gardens are reserved for the front approach and the drawing room (the most ceremonious parts of the house). Gyo, abridging some of the scenic details, is a somewhat less formal setting used for the dining or living areas, while So, the most abridged and asymmetrical form, overlooks the most retired parts of the house.

The degree of formality in each garden is reflected in the flowers in the tokonoma, and when the broad exterior panel slides back the interior of the house becomes an extension of the outdoor scene, giving a satisfying feeling of unity. If the garden suggests a plain, mountains and water are depicted in the tokonoma and vice versa. Material appearing in the garden and seen through the windows is not featured in the house.

In fact, few flowers have been cultivated other than in picking gardens since the seventeenth century; such blooms might detract from those in the tokonoma. Over-decoration is frowned upon as vulgar ostentation, while an indigenous growth (in both garden and tokonoma) is prized far above showy imports. Some schools still prohibit the use of hybrid blooms in interior or exterior designs, feeling they are too demanding in size and color to be in good taste.

A single flower arrangement and two other closely related objects of art such as a *kakemono* (a hanging scroll-shaped painting) and a piece of sculpture are usually displayed together in the tokonoma. And it hardly seems necessary to say that such objects are carefully selected to complement—not vie with—each other. Everything not essential or not appropriate to the setting is kept stored away. To be fully appreciated, beauty must be individually savored.

The kakemono often depicts a landscape, or a calligraphic scroll expressing some ethical teaching might be selected to hang beside the flower arrangement. Completing the trio, an incense burner or other decorative object might be carefully chosen. This group representing three fine arts—in the same close relationship first found on altars so many centuries ago—gives a note of quiet elegance to the tastefully chaste rooms.

Flowers in the tokonoma follow the natural laws of growth—turning away from the shade (blank wall) and "flowing" toward the southern sunlight of the garden. The lines of the arrangement reach out like a welcoming hand toward the guest of honor and lead his eye gently into the garden. Since the flower arrangement and outdoor scene complement each other, this area, as well as the occasion and the taste of a specially honored guest, is carefully considered in planning the design.

Entertaining guests before the tokonoma has played an indispensable part in Japanese home life since the early thirteenth century. However, no one enters the tokonoma and nothing untidy or unclean is ever placed in it—even temporarily.

Upon entering the room, a well-behaved guest sits quietly three feet from the tokonoma and bows gently; he first looks into the lower part of the arrangement, then glances upward. If he wishes to see the "roots and round about" he bows again, crawling quietly up to the tokonoma, then, resting hands on knees, "looks gently in, refraining from criticism or rough movement." Not until he has politely crawled back to the three-foot position is he free to speak or look elsewhere. Although he is expected to express admiration, exaggerated praise—which would not be in accord with the floral group—is considered bad taste.

The subtle harmony between garden, scroll, flowers, and single other art object is such a long-established tradition and its meaning so generally understood that a minimum of detail is called for in order to suggest a particular landscape, season, or idea. The plant material interprets the *spirit* of the time—gaiety and abundance for spring, simplicity and broad expanses of water to provide a feeling of coolness in summer, a touch of pathos to signify autumn, and hardy evergreens, grasses, and bare branches for winter.

Only flowers in season—or slightly in advance of season—are represented in either

Two separate groups of sansevieria cut to Ikenobo proportion and two slender-necked pottery swans (gazing soulfully at each other) are unified into a single composition entitled "Spring Song." The bird at the back rests on a block of wood behind the container and is placed so that the broadest part of its body is exposed to view. The bird in the foreground—of the same size—appears smaller only because it is turned at an angle which accentuates the slenderest lines.

The sleek, shiny texture and vivid greens of the plant material make a pleasant contrast to the dull, rough texture of the birds, container, and base. Leaves and shiny black pebbles cover the needlepoint holder. Each unit, arranged with clean-cut lines, contributes to the over-all circular feeling of the composition. The broad base provides necessary weight at the bottom of the design and helps create the illusion of an island nesting place to which the male bird has just brought a timid young mate. (Photo: Lawrence Joseph.)

the arrangement or the scroll painting, and no flower is displayed in front of its painted likeness. While some schools prescribe that the flowers should help illustrate the verse on a kakemono, others claim flowers should not be placed before a sonnet extolling their beauties, "lest the poem suffer by such a comparison."

If the kakemono shows a waterfall, the flower arrangement incorporates plants that grow in or near the water, and some ornament closely associated with water is selected as the third component part of the group. Or, during the wet season, a beautifully wrought replica of a hand drum (symbol of movement and ritual music) might be placed beneath the scroll to indicate the noise of the cataract swelled by rain.

In another mood the container itself might rest on a stand in the shape of the crest of a wave, or include a wave design, while water plants and a carving of a smiling Buddha would complete the harmonious ensemble.

Bamboo and sparrows are used to express loyalty, because of an old Chinese fable which tells of sparrows who, living in a bamboo fence surrounding the Emperor's palace, sounded the alarm whenever danger was at hand. (The song of the sparrow even resembles the Japanese word for loyalty.) When associated with the tiger, bamboo indicates safety, or a difficult mission accomplished, for the tiger's mortal enemy, the elephant, cannot harm him once he reaches the shelter of a bamboo grove.

Lions and peonies are at home together, for one is king of beasts and the other is queen of flowers. Maple and deer remind the observer of Nara, where the deer run undisturbed about the temple buildings. Plum blossoms and the nightingale have been happily associated in poetry, and scholars enjoy the frog and willow, whose special association with one another has been explained earlier in the book.

For wedding celebrations an arrangement of pine often includes a crane or tortoise, both of which express the wish for a long and hardy life. Or the figures of an old man and woman might be added to represent the spirits of the two pines of *Takasago* (a Noh, or "dance drama," in which, symbolically, the human experiences of the two trees are beautifully depicted). The pine represents loyalty to the Tenno, or Emperor, and is seldom neglected at a wedding.

Until very recently, however, few Japanese arrangements incorporated figures of men, birds, or animals. Accessories appeared only as a unit in the traditional groupings of kakemono and flowers, helping to create a unified picture within the frame of the tokonoma.

Many schools of Japanese flower arrangement were set up solely to guide students in the proper decoration of the tokonoma, and the traditions they set have remained unchanged for hundreds of years. Usubatas were designed with the tokonoma in mind (as were other traditional Japanese containers) and therefore an arrangement correctly proportioned to these containers was also properly scaled for its place of display.

The accepted placement of articles in the tokonoma called for the usual tridimensional approach. The area was divided into three imaginary parts and the arrangement was placed on the first or second division, according to the style of the flowers. Great care was taken in hanging the kakemono so that the artist was never discredited by flowers obscuring his signature. A suitable accessory was then placed so as to complete the asymmetrical grouping. The lines as well as the thought associations of the flower arrangement, the scroll, and the accessory lead to a fuller enjoyment of the beauty of each.

The tokonoma is never crowded and frequently it contains only a kakemono and flower arrangement. At least two-thirds of the alcove remains unoccupied, as a foil for beauty both real and implied. The proper distribution of free space will often relate widely varying art forms.

Construction Details for Incorporating Other Art Forms

1. *Selecting suitable forms.*

Incorporating other objects in floral compositions is not complicated, but it does entail a little more thought than a simple one-unit flower design.

A niche or frame—the Occidental equivalent of a tokonoma—will usually give a more pleasing effect if at least one-third of the area is left free. And the maximum height, width, and depth of the design (even when very delicate material is used) will usually prove more satisfactory if a clearance of at least one inch per foot is left free on all sides. In other words, a niche measuring four feet high, three feet wide, and two feet deep would call for material that was held at least four inches below the top of it, within at least three inches of each side, and two or more inches from the back wall and the front. A larger arrangement in the same space would look uncomfortably crowded.

After a careful study of the location and purpose for which the design is intended, there are four questions to consider:

(a) What materials will best express the theme or meaning?

(b) Will flowers or another art form dominate the scene?

(c) Can the idea be expressed with a single accessory or will it be necessary to incorporate additional objects?

(d) Are the chosen elements (including the container and available plant material) compatible with each other through association of idea, as well as through relationship of line, color, and texture?

2. *Placing the accessories.*

The word "accessory" is often misused, for it is not possible—as called for in some flower-show schedules—to "feature an accessory." Any object may be featured, but if it is, the object dominates the design and ceases to be an "accessory." In this chapter, one illustration features an elephant and one features birds, while in the compositions "Texas Tidelands" and "Moonlight and Shadow" birds and a hippopotamus represent accessories. These accessories help tell a story; they play an important but minor part in the design.

Every design should start with the placement of the main element. If flowers are to be featured, the container should be placed first, followed by the accessory or accessories. If a piece of sculpture or driftwood is to be featured, it should be placed first, establishing the best possible position and line to which all other elements in the design will be subordinated.

Any element being featured or any accessory should be in proper proportion to the over-all design, which should conform to these rules:

(a) All elements should be large enough to have meaning, but none so large as to overpower the design.

(b) The plant material should play an integral part in the lines of other art forms, repeating those lines and merging with them to lead the eye smoothly through the design.

(c) No form should be inappropriately used. (While waterbirds standing in water are logical, men, unless barefoot or wearing hip boots, are not.)

(d) As in a picture of any kind, interest will be heightened if all forms are placed so they help tell the story while completing the design.

3. *Final check.*

Regardless of what forms are being featured, a harmonious whole can be achieved only when all elements complement one another in idea, shape, proportion, color, and texture to form an integrated design. Each element must:

(a) contribute to the main lines of the design (diagram IX-A);

(b) be subordinate to the composition as a whole and related to the other elements (diagram IX-B);

(c) give a feeling of stability and help draw the eye, by rhythmic repetition, down through the logical story which is depicted (diagram IX-C).

The weight of the chunky bronze container and the vertical thrust of the weathered wood stabilize the movement of the elephant and spiraling rain lilies in this highly stylized design entitled "The Rain Forest."

The irregularly shaped plaque adds to the feeling of depth and movement as the elephant steps up onto the plateau for his "meal." (Photo: Lawrence Joseph.)

In "Parade of Champions" the mare seems to be instructing her reluctant colt, while the stallion stands behind, with head thrown back and forefeet in the shallow water hole beneath the tree.

In spite of the number and conspicuous gold-yellow coloring of the horses, their careful arrangement as a single unit keeps them from overpowering the design. The eye is led rhythmically along their heads and up into the heart of the design, with its classic Shin, Soe, and Tai proportions.

The analogous color scheme is made up of yellow and browns with a bright touch of orange provided by the glazed lining of the container. Rough textures found in the container, rocks, and windblown tree contrast with the sleek surfaces of the pottery horses and the rosewood plaque. (Photo: Lawrence Joseph.)

"Texas Tidelands" is a free Moribana interpretation. The swamp-palmetto "gusher" maintains the three prescribed levels and proportions, while the native irises growing from the curved tree trunk at its feet reach diagonally across the container to tie the various elements together. The weathered, pecky cypress container, placed on a slab of dull black glass, contributes to the illusion of a brackish setting for the swamp-loving birds.

The plant material is placed at the back of the container with stems swinging well out over the front; the accessories start behind the container and follow the same forward movement. These placements add depth (implied as well as real) and impart an additional touch of realism to the miniature landscape scene. (Photo: *New York Times.*)

"Moonlight and Shadow"—a study in black and white—places great emphasis on texture. Rough textures are used in the light areas, smooth textures in the dark parts of the design such as the glossy black base bneath the hippopotamus which suggests dark jungle water.

Ecru mushrooms (cured in borax) "grow" among the darkened magnolia foliage. The leaves were cured in a mixture of glycerine and liquid black shoe polish which deepened the veining and gave them a soft, shadowy, exotic look.

The main lines of the chalk-white tree are repeated in the sleek black "shadow" branch which curls downward over the back of the hippo and creates a pleasing contrast in color and motion.

Fresh magnolia leaves and white narcissi might be substituted for the mushrooms and treated leaves, thus starting the design off in the spring with flowers that could be easily changed as the seasons progressed. (Photo: Lawrence Joseph.)

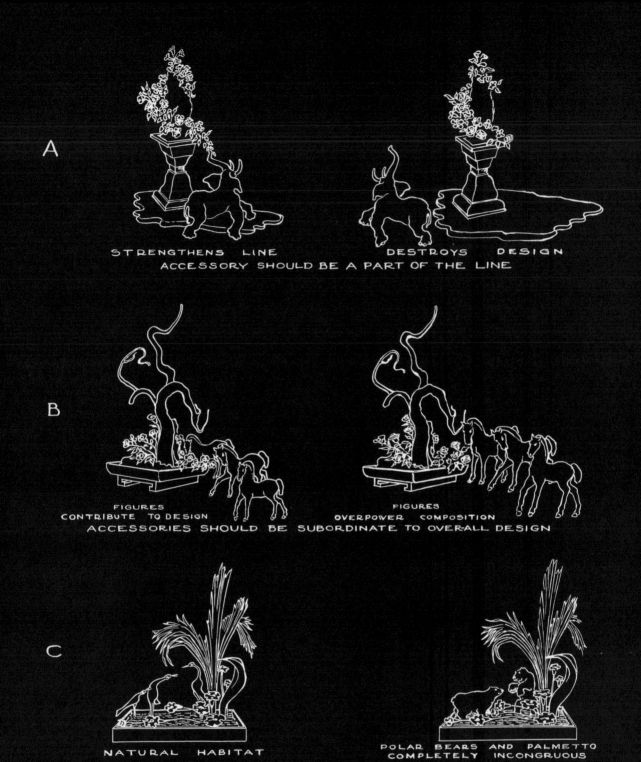

A

STRENGTHENS LINE   DESTROYS DESIGN
ACCESSORY SHOULD BE A PART OF THE LINE

B

FIGURES
CONTRIBUTE TO DESIGN   FIGURES
OVERPOWER COMPOSITION
ACCESSORIES SHOULD BE SUBORDINATE TO OVER-ALL DESIGN

C

NATURAL HABITAT   POLAR BEARS AND PALMETTO
COMPLETELY INCONGRUOUS
ACCESSORIES SHOULD TELL A LOGICAL STORY

DIAGRAM IX

IX: Japanese Adaptations for Contemporary Settings

Much magazine and newspaper space is devoted daily to various phases of home furnishing. Hundreds of books have been written on the subject. Everything from hanging pictures to scientific lighting and the psychological effect of color has been presented; and almost every photograph pertaining to home, club, or even office decor includes some kind of floral material.

Both professional decorators and discriminating homemakers lean heavily upon nature for that final lift—the ultimate warmth—in a room. However, this important note in the decorative scheme is often casually put together and carelessly placed.

Men of vision in many countries actually design rooms around waterfalls, giant trees, huge boulders, or other natural phenomena; and even conservative architects now feature indoor plantings and treat surrounding views as part of the interior design.

The new feeling of space and freedom from extraneous decoration calls for simple, well-executed floral designs, an art which the Japanese have been practicing for hundreds of years.

The principles taught by the Japanese are helpful in arranging flowers for any setting. Irrespective of the type of architecture, the main objective in any decorative scheme is to relate and complement the objects in each room. Regardless of whether the over-all design features a fine painting, the view, a piece of sculpture, or the floral arrangement itself, everything should blend to emphasize and lead the eye toward this feature.

The Japanese realize how difficult it is to achieve harmony unless the floral design is actually created in the location for which it is intended. Therefore, in spite of the neutral backgrounds and uniform size of the setting, flowers are arranged in front of the tokonoma. Provisions for this on-the-spot construction include trays for holding plant material and tools as well as a square of cloth for protecting the floor or matting. (Specific dimensions for this item vary from forty inches square to twenty-two and one-

A Nageire arrangement of yellow roses and mahonia finds a happy setting in the corner of a traditional American living room. The eye is led from the chair to the arrangement and through it to the Chippendale tray and elegant lacquered table on top of the secretary. The entire composition is pleasingly framed by the Williamsburg-pattern draperies and a handsome burl adds necessary weight and importance to the flower arrangement.

Treated with glycerine, the mahonia could become a permanent background, and the roses could be replaced with any appropriate yard-grown flowers as the seasons progressed. (Photo: John Hugelmeyer.)

Two pale-blue iris blossoms contrast beautifully with the grayed-shell-pink shiki-silk bedroom wall. The double-rooted design appears here in a pair of Sung bowls instead of in a single flat container. The bowl containing the Shin and Soe groups is placed on a second stand to give it additional importance and both bowls share the same large base—an effective device for tying a design together.

Japanese arrangers seldom show a full-blown blossom in the Soe group (since Soe is on the north); if two blooms were used they would appear in slightly different stages of development, with one as part of the Shin group and the other in the Tai group. However, this liberty was taken so that the maximum amount of blue would appear against the pink wall. (Photo: Gottscho-Schleisner.)

This arrangement in an antique bronze usubata is an integral part of the decor of the room and, at the time the photograph was taken, had just celebrated its tenth birthday!

Celosia stems dry as satisfactorily as the blooms and here several different plants have been used to create a "tree." The celosia stems were soaked in warm water until they were soft enough to mold into interesting shapes; they were then joined together with waterproof glue. (Pins held the stems together until the glue set.) Fresh celosia blooms and stems may be added at will and the entire tree can be washed whenever necessary (to remove dust). Celosia will keep its color indefinitely. The blooms are merely pinned and glued to hold their positions. (Photo: Gottscho-Schleisner, Inc.)

half inches square, according to the school.) These articles are as routine as the container and flowers themselves.

In Japan the lower line of the design is placed to lead the eye into the garden. In Occidental settings this line may be used to strengthen the effect by reaching out welcomingly toward the entrance door, or it may lead the eye to a picture, the couch, the fireplace, a piece of prized furniture, or any other outstanding feature of the room. Once design principles are mastered, the height of an Occidental adaptation is easily adjusted to the proportions of the room as a whole, and the colors blended to complement existing colors.

Containers for this type of design should act as a foil for the plant material and be in keeping with the other furnishings through texture and general feeling. They should be selected to complement the beauty of the setting in which they are placed. The entire design should be related to everything in the room and should—like a painting—be "hung" neither too high nor too low. Thus, by employing the simplicity and restraint of feeling practiced by the Oriental in the use of flowers, arrangements can be made that will add charm and grace to any type of room.

The colors of available floral material (as well as the room as a whole) should be studied both at night and in the daytime. And the actual shape of the free space which will act as a background or frame for the design should be carefully considered. The general plan or shape of the arrangement (in relation to the boundaries of this free area), should then be roughed in on paper, no matter how crudely.

Once a satisfactory pattern is developed for a specific location it is easily repeated with different material throughout the year. No two arrangements are ever identical, and yet the underlying framework or basic shape and best style fitted to a particular setting can be repeated with distinction in each new composition.

Year-round suggestions for the use of floral material are encountered in gardens and on roadsides, while new ideas may be found in magazines, books, paintings, Chinese and Japanese prints, and flower shows. Above all, nature teaches us the fundamentals of design through the growing habits of flowers and trees. By concentrated study of them the Japanese evolved a scientific approach to the art of arranging flowers which we can easily adapt to our particular needs. Since everyone sees differently and expresses what he sees in his own individual manner, the practice of following the patterns set up by Japanese flower masters does not eliminate originality.

Interpreting the fleeting beauty of nature's cycles not only develops a dynamic style of arranging but soon becomes a vital part of living. Such designs reflect both the essence of nature and the dignity of man.

Shin, Soe, and Tai lines are clearly defined by the three Picardy gladioli and foliage arranged in a horizontal container. The lines of the arrangement emphasize the vertical room dividers, and carry the observer's attention pleasantly from the exotic plant in the foyer.

Glass slag covers the needlepoint holder, giving weight at the base of the design and additional elegance to the translucent plastic container. (Photo: Gottscho-Schleisner.)

A silver container arranged with five callas and two leaves. The design is placed on a black teakwood stand to balance the forward movement of the large flowers. Six black candles (in graduated lengths) set in silver holders complete the composition.

The wall design behind the arrangement features a cherry tree, and in season cherry blossoms would be a logical choice for this contemporary dining-room setting. Cherry blossoms symbolize feminine beauty and purity, as well as chivalry and knightly honor; they are also the symbol of the Japanese people. (As the bloom is subordinate to the whole, so do the people subordinate their individuality to the glory of the nation. The tree breaks suddenly into beauty and as suddenly the blossoms scatter—the tree melts into its surroundings. So does the Samurai answer the call of duty and die—without murmuring or lingering.)

In order to counteract thoughts of death the Ikenobo masters added a small branch of mountain pine to arrangements of cherry blossoms (showing that the tree grows on mountaintops), but no other tree or flower is sanctioned with cherry. It is not even used in the same room with other flowers and, when displayed in flower shows, occupies a higher level than other arrangements—a silent tribute to the undisputed king of the flower realm. (Photo: Gottscho-Schleisner, Inc.)

Gnarled oak branches adapted to a double-rooted kan-suike (water-viewing) design add interest to the frosted glass recess which contains air-conditioning ducts, stereophonic speakers, and other mechanical devices. The Moribana arrangement (on the television cabinet—see page 71 for close-up) incorporates cattails, thus furthering the illusion of a tree reaching across the water.

Several limbs were combined to make the composite "tree." Leaves (treated with glycerine and green cake coloring before being sprayed with fire-proofing compound) were then attached to the limbs with wire. The diffused green of the leaves picks up the soft, grayed moss-green in carpet and ceiling, while floodlights (controlled by rheostat) behind the frosted glass produce moonlight, twilight, or full sunlight effects with a flick of the switch.

The "perpetual" design, protected by the glass, needs neither dusting nor replacements and lends a dramatic note to what would otherwise have been an unsightly but necessary detail in the contemporary apartment.

The Moribana arrangement on the cabinet provides pleasing seasonal changes and helps point up the duality of life—the changing and unchanging verities of the universe. (Photo: Gottscho-Schleisner, Inc.)

details of frosted glass tree

FLOWERS REPRESENTING
THE MONTHS OF THE YEAR IN JAPAN

JANUARY: *prune blossom*

FEBRUARY: *peach blossom*

MARCH: *tree peony*

APRIL: *cherry blossom*

MAY: *magnolia*

JUNE: *pomegranate blossom*

JULY: *lotus flower*

AUGUST: *pear blossom*

SEPTEMBER: *mallow*

OCTOBER: *chrysanthemum*

NOVEMBER: *gardenia*

DECEMBER: *poppy*

GUIDE TO PRONUNCIATION

(Japanese pronunciations, like those of other languages, vary with the locale. Those applying to terminology employed in this book have been worked out after consultations with people from various parts of the country. For words about which there was a definite difference of opinion, both pronunciations are shown.)

bonsai (bon-sigh)
boku (bo-koo)
Chabana (char-bar-nar or chah-bah-nah)
dai (die)
do (doe)
Enshiu (arn-she-oou or eng-shoo)
Gyo (guy-o)
Iemoto (i-ee-mo-toe or ee-eh-mo-toe)
ikebana (ik-ee-bar-nar or ee-keh-baa-nah)
Ikenobo (ik-ee-no-bo or ee-keh-no-bo)
kago (car-go)
Kakebana (car-key-bar-nar)
kakemono (car-key-mo-no)
kansuike (can-soo-ee-keh or
    karn-soo-ee-keh)
kenzin (ken-zin)
komi (ko-mee)

kubari (koo-bar-ee)
matagi (mat-ah-ghi)
Moribana (mo-ree-bar-nar)
Morimono (mo-ree-mo-no)
Nageire (nah-gay-ee-ray)
nejime (nay-gee-may or nay-chee-meh)
nemoto (nay-mo-toe)
Rikkwa (rick-war or rich-ah)
sabi (sar-bee)
samurai (sam-you-rye or sa-moo-rah-ee)
Shin-no-hana (shin-no-har-nar or
    shin-no-haa-nah)
Soe (soy)
Tai (tie)
tokonoma (toe-ko-no-mar)
tome (toe-may)
usubata (use-uh-bar-tar or oo-suh-bar-tar)

BIBLIOGRAPHY

Ball, Katherine M. *Decorative Motives of Oriental Art.* New York: Dodd, Mead, 1927.

Binyon, Laurence, and Sexton, J. J. O. *Japanese Colour Prints,* New York: Scribner, 1923.

Binyon, Laurence. *Painting in the Far East.* New York: Longmans, Green, 1924.

Blossfeldt, Karl. *Art Forms in Nature.* New York: E. Weyhe, 1929.

Brod, Fritzi. *Flowers in Nature and Design.* New York: Stephen Daye Press, 1947.

Conder, Josia. *The Flowers of Japan and the Art of Japanese Floral Arrangements.* New York: 1889; second edition imported by Scribner, 1902.

Dewey, John. *Art as Experience.* New York: Minton, Balch, 1934.

Feldsted, Carol J. *Design Fundamentals.* New York: Pitman Publications, 1951.

Fenollosa, Ernest F. *Epochs of Chinese and Japanese Art.* New York: Frederick A. Stokes, 1921.

Ficke, Arthur Davison. *Chats on Japanese Prints.* New York: Frederick A. Stokes, 1915.

Goldstein, Harriet, Irene, and Vetta. *Art in Everyday Life.* New York: Macmillan, 1925.

Gorham, Hazel H., and Oshikawa, Josui. *Correspondence Course in Japanese Flower Arrangement.* Tokyo: The New Osaka Building, Uchisaiwai-Cho, Kojimach-Ku, Nippon Bunka Renmei, 1940.

Hanono, Seizabara Mishikawa. *Japanese Art of Flower Arrangements.* Japan: Shiori Sha Kohoto, n.d.

Hawley, W. M. *Chinese Folk Design.* Hollywood, California: W. M. Hawley, 1949.

Iwata, Seido. *Japanese Flower Arrangement.* New York: Studio Publications, Inc., 1954.

Koehn, Alfred. *Japanese Flower Symbolism.* Tokyo: at the Lotus Court, 1954.

Koehn, Alfred. *Way of Japanese Flower Arrangement.* Tokyo: Kyo Bun Kwan, second edition, 1937.

Morrison, Arthur. *The Painters of Japan.* New York: Frederick A. Stokes, n.d.

Newsom, Samuel. *A Thousand Years of Japanese Gardens.* Tokyo: News Service, second revised edition, 1955.

Ohashi, S. *Japanese Floral Arrangement.* New York: Yamanaka and Co., 1935.

Oshikawa, Josui, and Gorham, Hazel H. *Manual of Japanese Flower Arrangement.* New York: Stechert, 1936.

Runes, D. D., and Schrickel, H. G. *Encyclopedia of the Arts.* New York: Philosophical Library, 1945.

Sansom, George Bailey. *Japan: A Short Cultural History.* New York: Century, 1931.

Shoji, Kane, and Johnson, V. M. *The Japanese Principles of Design in Flower Arrangement.* Seattle: The Chieftain Press, 1950.

Tamura, Tsuyoshi. *Art of the Landscape Garden in Japan.* New York: Dodd, Mead, 1936.

Tsujii, Koshu. *Moribana and Heikwa; Selected Flower Arrangements of the Saga School.* London: Routledge and Kegan Paul, 1933.

Tsujii, Koshu. *The Mastery of Japanese Flower Arrangement.* Translated by Jogaku and Fujii. Rutland, Vermont: Charles E. Tuttle Company, 1940.

Yoshida, Tetsuro. *The Japanese House and Garden.* New York: Frederick A. Praeger, 1955.